ANNE CROSSMAN'S

COMMONPLACE

BOOK

Anne Crossman's Commonplace Book
—© 2025 Anne Crossman

Cover design: Rebekah Wetmore, from a photograph by Albert Rice
Editor: Andrew Wetmore

ISBN: 978-1-998149-89-6
First edition July, 2025

Moose House Publications
2475 Perotte Road
Annapolis County, NS B0S 1A0
moosehousepress.com
info@moosehousepress.com

Moose House Publications recognizes the support of the Province of Nova Scotia. We are pleased to work in partnership with the Department of Communities, Culture and Heritage to develop and promote our cultural resources for all Nova Scotians.

NOVA SCOTIA
NOUVELLE-ÉCOSSE

We live and work in Mi'kma'ki, the ancestral and unceded territory of the Mi'kmaw people. This territory is covered by the "Treaties of Peace and Friendship" which Mi'kmaw and Wolastoqiyik (Maliseet) people first signed with the British Crown in 1725. The treaties did not deal with surrender of lands and resources but in fact recognized Mi'kmaq and Wolastoqiyik (Maliseet) title and established the rules for what was to be an ongoing relationship between nations. We are all Treaty people.

Foreword

I have never considered myself a writer. But much of my working life has involved writing in one form or another. I think words became important to me when I was given books for Christmas presents when I was a child, and I devoured them. Then, too, my mother was a prodigious letter writer. She kept the family updated as we all moved around the country and the world. Her family were letter writers, too. and her brother had a weekly newspaper in Beamsville, Ontario. He wrote small books on subjects as varied as soccer and the islands of Saint Pierre and Miquelon. So my small columns each week come from a history of words.

I have never written long; always short. There have been times when I wrote so short as to be incomprehensible. Those who know me will find this a bit funny, as I can hold forth at length on almost any subject at the drop of a hat—verbally, out loud.

In the fall of 2020, Ashley Thompson, then editor of the Saltwire weekly newspaper *Annapolis Valley Register*, asked if I would be interested in doing a weekly column. After a thoughtful 30 seconds, I agreed —with gusto.

Every week since November, 2020 I have sent off my thoughts on all kinds of subjects, making sure the column went out on Sunday evening. Then I would wait until Thursday morning to see my column on the editorial page. My editor changed during that time to Jason Malloy.

The reason I am starting off with the editors is that they were delightful to work with. While it didn't happen very often, when they very gently suggested a change, they were always correct.

Editors are a rare breed. They can be brutal but right; they can also make you feel like a kid in grade 1. I have never had a hint of that with these two lovely people. They got me on the page both in print and digitally every week. And I owe this book to them.

I have lived in many different parts of Canada over time, and in Luxembourg for three years many years ago. Each of the places has given me something new to think about. Every now and then a news item or a piece in a book or magazine will remind me of somewhere I lived or visited, and I marvel that I have had such a wide variety of experiences.

I have met such a great bunch of people along the way, many of whom I still hear from.

The lovely people at Moose House Publications—Brenda J. Thompson and Andrew Wetmore—have been so gracious to take this book on, and I can't thank them enough.

And so, this book is dedicated to my partner, Bill, who went with me on most of my journey; to my daughters, Krista and Holly, who put up with me; and to their children and their children's children. It is also dedicated to all the lovely people in my life who helped make it so interesting. And I also want to dedicate this book to my country. I am so lucky to have been, and be, a Canadian person.

AC
May, 2025

These columns originally appeared in publications of the SaltWire Network, and are republished here with their graceful permission.

Anne Crossman's Commonplace Book

Anne Crossman's Commonplace Book

Anne Crossman's

Memories

Writing is a solitary craft. It comes from something inside that makes its way onto my screen.

I have lived quite a long time—longer than my parents did and longer than my grandparents. Memories pop up once in a while, and if I think that bit of my mind is still interesting, on that screen it goes.

Anne Crossman's

When we remember: doors to the past

November 12, 2020

In 1994, I received my father's[1] flight logs from his time in World War II. I also had some of my mother's[2] diaries from the same time. I had just retired, my mother had passed away a few months previously and I needed something to keep me busy and engrossed—something useful and meaningful.

I transcribed the three log books and the diaries and linked them together chronologically. The work gave me a glimpse into my parents' lives from 1938 through January, 1945.

Dad took flying lessons at the Ottawa Flying Club in 1938, went to England to join the Royal Air Force in the spring of 1939 and flew light bombers; and then in 1942 started flying Spitfires. My mother went to England in early 1940, married my father, and had me in Chester. The whole story is told in some detail in a blog I started in 2009[3].

Collecting all the information on my parents' time during World War II was an adventure. I found information and friends in abundance. I travelled to England and Belgium. I remembered small bits and pieces that became links to other bits and pieces.

And the links continued amongst family members too. My cousins had a relationship with the Thomas Fisher Rare Book Library of the University of Toronto. They wondered if I knew what was going to happen to all the memorabilia I had collected along with the information. I had been wondering that as well. Long story short – I was able to send all the material off to the library and they

---

1   W/C Philip V.K. Tripe
2   Elizabeth (Rannie) Tripe
3   philtripe.blogspot.com

were delighted to have it.

Two weeks ago, I received an email from the Special Collections Librarian who has written an article for the Fisher Library bi-annual publication, *The Halcyon*[4], about my collection. I would like to quote from this article and then you can read the whole piece for yourselves.

> Philip's logbooks, and Elizabeth's diaries, along with the photographs, telegrams and physical objects, such as the GQ club pin, Philip's hat badge and buttons, and of course, the pieces of his destroyed Spitfire, make the war and the personal experiences of the Tripes all the more tangible and accessible. This multifaceted collection has already proven to be effective with students, who have expressed their fascination with the items in classes held last fall. This archival collection is a compelling example of the historical and research value of personal experiences of historical events and joins the growing collections of World War II material at the Fisher, which will be preserved and available for teaching, exhibitions and research in the future.
>
> *– Danielle Van Wagner, Special Collections Librarian,*
> *Thomas Fisher Rare Book Library, University of Toronto*

I couldn't be more proud.

---

4   fisher.library.utoronto.ca/publications/halcyon

The mysterious Marie Celeste

November 26, 2020

The 'Today in History' columns in *The Chronicle-Herald* newspaper over time have yielded some fascinating tidbits of information. This one turned up in October, 2020:

> November 10, 1872 Cargo ship Mary Celeste sails from Staten Island for Genoa; mysteriously found abandoned four weeks later.

It triggered a lovely wistful time for me when I was honoured to help edit for reprinting, a wonderful book written by Peggy Armstrong (1929-2019) and researched by Marguerite Wagner, *Age of Sail*. The book has a gripping story about the Marie Celeste.

> Out of all the vessels built at Bear River, the most intriguing story is that of the 296-ton brigantine *Dei Gratia* and her involvement in one of the greatest unsolved sea mysteries of all time.
>
> What happened to Captain Benjamin Briggs and the crew of the American brigantine *Mary Celeste*? Why was the vessel abandoned so hastily on November 25, 1872, while proceeding from New York to Genoa with 1,700 barrels of alcohol in the hold? What was the fate of the captain's wife and young daughter? This mystery became the inspiration for countless newspaper articles, several books and numerous theories ranging all the way from murder, mutiny and piracy through to collusion and insurance hoax.
>
> The ill-fated voyage of the *Mary Celeste* got under way on November 10, 1872, when she cleared New York for Genoa, Italy. Five days later, the *Dei Gratia*, Captain David Reed Morehouse, left New York for Gibraltar with a cargo of petroleum and an eight-man crew on board. On December 5, the *Dei Gratia* was

mid-way between the Azores and Cabo da Roca, Portugal, when the crew sighted a vessel drifting aimlessly about under reduced canvas. On closer inspection, the derelict proved to be the *Mary Celeste.*

After hailing the brigantine and receiving no response, Captain Morehouse sent his first mate, Oliver Deveau, and two other seamen to board her.

It immediately became evident that the *Mary Celeste* had been completely abandoned.

There is quite the story about this abandoned vessel on Wikipedia.

Peggy was a bright, lively, smart, and funny woman. It was always a delight to visit her and find out where all the bits and pieces of the book (the original manuscript and photos) were and what changes needed to be made. *Age of Sail* was first self-published in 2001 and was out of print by 2017. The Annapolis Heritage Society believed that it was important enough to have it reprinted, and I volunteered to see the work done.

There are some rip-roaring tales in this book, and I was taken with the details of the ships that were built in Annapolis County back in the day. I have a few other favourites which I will regale you with as time goes by.

You can still buy Peggy's book at the O'Dell House Museum in Annapolis Royal.

Christmas around Canada

December 24, 2020

Many years ago, I used to get books and a purse from my "aunts" and my godmother in Chester, England. The purses were little, with woven embroidery thread handles and lovely painted designs on the front. The books started with the "Noddy" books by Enid Blyton and, as I grew older, The "Famous Five" detective books. I waited eagerly for those gifts each Christmas for many years and had that year's books devoured by New Year's Day.

Time moved on and I started getting holiday clothes and sometimes books—*Black Beauty, Old Black Joe, The Secret Garden*. Many of you will remember those.

My Christmases changed when my family moved to Luxembourg in the 50s (Dad was in the RCAF and posted to a NATO base in Trier, Germany). The festivities there begin on December 6, when Saint Nicholas (Kleeschen) comes to Echternach on a barge down the Sauer River. He arrives at the town square with candies for the good children, and Housécker, the Christmas bogeyman, has a birch switch for the bad boys and girls. And on Christmas Eve, the tradition was that a gift from the Christ Child was opened after mass in the lovely St. Willibrord Basilica.

So the holiday stretched out over almost the whole month of December.

I have counted the number of Christmases I have spent since returning to Canada and the different places: 16! From Newfoundland and Labrador to New Brunswick to Quebec to the Northwest Territories to Nunavut to British Columbia to Saskatchewan to Alberta to Ontario to Nova Scotia, I spent Christmases in good times and in some hard times. I realize how fortunate I am to have lived all over this country and to have met so many really nice people.

If I were to pick a few good holiday memories, these are the ones.

- Helping my parents decorate the tree on Christmas Eve after the younger ones were sent to bed on the RCAF base at St. Hubert, QC.
- Making my first tourtière from Helen Gougeon's cookbook—a lovely Christmas present.
- Having a Norwegian Christmas Eve dinner with our neighbours on the Bauline Line in Portugal Cove, NL. And being at a party that the Mummers visited in St. John's, NF.
- Driving out to find a Christmas tree in Yellowknife, NT, finding one, chopping it down and hearing all the needles go "tinkle, tinkle" as they dropped off onto the frozen ground, and having the car not start when we got back to the road. It was -40° C and we had to wait until some part of the engine warmed up enough. That was a "Charlie Brown" Christmas tree, for sure.
- Going to the Caribou Carnival in Yellowknife, the kids having some candies in some kind of cellophane bag which just shattered into a gazillion pieces in the -30° C. weather.
- Having the absolute best Christmas tree in Prince Rupert, BC, a

    lodgepole pine found in a swamp with, some extra branches poked into holes drilled into the trunk. It was picture-perfect.

- Being in Inuvik, NT when the sun went down on December 6 and came back up on January 6, with us down on the ice off the Mackenzie River with fireworks. They were paid for by the feds and meant for Canada Day. It was 24-hour daylight on July 1st, which would have made the fireworks pale imitations of themselves so we set them off to welcome back the sun in January.
- Being invited to our great neighbours for Christmas Eve dinner a couple of weeks after we landed in Annapolis County.
- Not to forget our first New Year's Eve here in Centrelea, at our other neighbours' with bridge tables and a punch that brought tears to one's eyes.
- And the time the shotgun was brought out to bring in the New Year and somehow the clothesline got in the way—here in Centrelea.

With this bit of writing, I send you all warm wishes for this cold but festive time of year. As we have been taught by all those terrific Public Health people this year: be safe, and, above all else, be kind.

Books and blogs

December 31, 2020

My life with reading began when most kids begin—around 3, 4 or 5. And, as for many, the big influence for me was my mother. She read and she read and she bought me books. I got books as Christmas presents.

    When I was in school in Ottawa, I went to the Kent Street Public Library at least once a week. I can still remember wondering what book to take out, and if nothing struck my fancy, I would take *Grimm's Fairy Tales* home and delight in those stories that took me to magical places. That book was first published in 1812.

    I devoured books and then newspapers and some magazines over time. I wrote letters home after leaving the nest to keep my folks up to date.

When I got into the news business, one of my favourite parts of it was doing the research. Delving into the bowels of documents and libraries and archives would take me to places I had no idea existed.

Some favourite stories from those days were doing research for a CBC-TV documentary on Samuel Cunard and tying it to the opening of the Come By Chance Refinery in Newfoundland. I spent days at the old Chase Building, where the Nova Scotia Archives resided back in the day. It was quite fascinating going through the old documents—nothing was digitized in those days!

I had to learn about the migratory habits of the different caribou herds in Northern Canada when I worked for a weekly newspaper in Yellowknife, *News of the North*. And I met and interviewed members of many of the First Nations and Inuit hunting organizations while there.

Doing the research on the Tsimshian Nation on British Columbia's northern coast for the Northwest Museum was fascinating. The museum wanted to change its whole structure and tell the story of the area from pre-European times to the present day.

I realize how lucky I am to have been able to read and learn about such a varied selection of pieces of information. I also remember learning to my shock about people I've known who couldn't read.

There was the really nice woman who would come once a week and clean my house and keep me company before I went to "work outside the home." I had no idea that her reading and writing skills were so low because she told great stories. Then, one day she left me note on some things she needed. I could hardly make out what she wanted. I was young and didn't know how to help, or even if she wanted help.

And then there was the fellow who knew he needed help. He went to classes when he was in his 40s. It made me weep when he proudly made his announcement at a party and showed us his first "story" that had been printed in a little booklet at the end of the class.

And we come to today's online world. I used to follow quite a few blogs. Now I have to be selective or I'd be in front of my screen more than I am now. I read a wonderful 'Letter to Americans' by Heather Cox Richardson, my good friend Bob Maher's 'Ernest Blair Experiment', and all my newspapers online as well.

I now have a Kobo e-reader, so my "real" books tend to pile up. I have a stack of four books waiting to be read, plus at least two that I am reading on the Kobo. It's kind of an interesting collection. The "real" book stack has Silver Donald Cameron's last book, *Blood in the Water*; Noah Richler's *Fear and Loathing on the Campaign Trail* (my husband bought that one); *Spitfire* by John Nichol; and *Rage* by Bob Woodward. The e-reader has *The Evening and the Morning* by Ken Follett and Barak Obama's latest book, *A Promised Land*.

When I look at the list, I realize I have enough reading material to get me (possibly) through the COVID pandemic.

And so we are at the end of 2020. And a good thing, too. While I expect the first part of this next year won't be a picnic, there seems to be some hope across the world. I wish everyone good health, good thoughts, safety and warmth. I also wish you stories to educate you and take you away to other places for a while.

And, above all else, in the words of a number of our senior medical people, be kind.

Happy New Year.

Channelling Queen Anne

February 4, 2021

Eleven years ago this week, on February 6, 2010, there was an auspicious gathering at the then-Annapolis Royal Golf and Country Club to celebrate the 345th birthday of Queen Anne. I know because I was there, as "Queen Anne".

Portraying a queen was, surprisingly, a lot of fun. As the plans for the 300th anniversary of the naming of Annapolis Royal moved along and I volunteered to help out, I found myself saying, "Oh, sure, I'd love to portray Queen Anne!"

The planning team was spectacular. I had a Royal Household with me during the year's events—Sarah Churchill, the Duchess of Marlborough; two footmen; a coachman (oh, yes, there was a coach); a costumière; a court jester; and various other hangers-on.

I kept a blog going at the time[5], mostly so I could remember the whirl-

---

5   mylifeasqueenanne.blogspot.com

wind of that year. You can read all the details, should you wish. I would like to highlight here the parts that were very funny, and some that were quite moving.

There was the time that our costumière had to measure the coachman for his costume and the banter that went on in his kitchen with his lovely wife looking on was hysterical. That guy kept the duchess and me laughing every time he was involved, with his lovely carriage and Bonnie, the dear mare.

We went in the Lawrencetown Exhibition Parade—the carriage, the coachman, the duchess, two footmen and me. As we drove down the main drag sort of among the miniature horses (which Bonnie the mare wasn't really sure about), the coachman was waving away to people and they were waving back and talking to him. And he would turn around and say, "Who the heck was that? I can't see them and I can't quite hear them!" And he'd wave again.

The duchess and I were in stitches the whole time. There was a big bump getting into the arena and there was much applause AND we won a beautiful red ribbon for Judge's Choice First Prize.

We met the Lt. Governor, Mayann Francis. That event at Fort Anne was very ceremonial and when "God Save the Queen" started up, I had a dilemma—do I stand or not? The Lt. Governor stood and I saw a bit of a flurry by her equerry out of the corner of my eye, but I decided to stay in the part and sat there. Fortunately, no one said anything afterwards.

We had our picture taken by some German tourists who thought we were just great.

There were tea parties. And we went to Upper Clements Park, to that lovely bandstand. One of my favourite moments was when a little girl came up very shyly to the bandstand and said in a tiny little voice, "I really like your dress, Queen." Nearly did me in, I tell you.

There were the times we were in the Annapolis Royal Town Hall getting changed into our garb. The boys were upstairs in the council chambers and occasionally one would holler down to ask where his other stocking was. The girls were downstairs in the CAO's office, with the blinds drawn, getting tied into various layers and getting that wig on straight. The laughter was just wonderful.

I really want to give credit where credit is due. Linda Brown was our "director"; Amery Boyer was Sarah Churchill, Duchess of Marlborough; Raymond Longley was our coachman; Jon Percy was a footman, as were Wayne Currie and David Stairs,;John Coker was the court jester; Ken Nye played the Privy-Counsellor and helped with the costumes; and the wonderful Millie Hawes made some of the most spectacular costumes for the production.

Learning about this little-known Queen who gave her name to Annapolis Royal and Annapolis County was a real education. She was both a tragic figure and, in her own way, an important figure in that time long ago and far away.

I wouldn't have missed that year for anything—even with the wretched, itchy wig, the slippery golden shoes, the crown which constantly threatened to fall off, the petticoat that always seemed to slip and the layers of material in a very warm summer. I do know that we all had a great time and hope that our audience enjoyed it as well.

Happy 356th birthday, Anne Regina!

Fireworks in the dark

April 29, 2021

Northern Canada starts in one's mind anywhere north of Edmonton or Saskatoon or Prince George. If you pull up Google Maps, you will know what I mean.

Going from Regina to La Ronge in Saskatchewan was North for me. La Ronge is a small community on the edge of Lac La Ronge. It had been a trading post for the Cree and Chipewyan people for years.

I was given the job of radio producer for the CBC there. We were a small but mighty crew, with our office and studio over Robertson Trading Post store. We had bay windows overlooking the dock for canoes, motorboats and float planes.

I mention the windows because studios in other CBC locations tended to be like bunkers. I can't you tell the delight I had when we were on the air and one of those Beaver float planes took off or landed. Anyone who has heard one will know that the window flexed and the music was turned up sooner than expected to drown out that engine.

I also lived in Inuvik (go to your map again) for almost ten years. We broadcast in English, Gwich'in, Inuvialuktun and Sahtúgot'įné Yatį (spoken by the Sahtu Dene). By the time I left, we were like a United Nations, with Northern First Nations people, a Southern First Nations person, an Egyptian and some non-First Nations people mixed in. It was somewhat of a training ground for some Southern people in news and current affairs. I keep in touch with some of these amazing people.

Some of my favourite memories from that time include our Spring River Breakup afternoon radio programs done by the Mackenzie River, where we served tea, did our programming AND the ice broke while we were on the air.

There was the time that a couple of our newsies took the station Chevy Blazer on the ice road to Tuktoyaktuk. These new-from-the-South ladies were given a bit of a lesson on driving on the ice road. As in, turning a corner is tricky, very tricky. Well, they did and went swooshing into the frozen snow bank. No injuries, except the Blazer was a bit dented as I recall, but it gave us stories to regale ourselves with for quite a while through the dark winter.

Speaking of dark winter, Inuvik is above the Arctic Circle. That means that it was pretty dark for a month from early December to early January. There were various reactions to this by the Southern people. We sort of kept an eye on them to make sure they were okay. If they were not, they got sent South on any pretext to get their fill of light. We did, eventually, put a sunlamp in the staff room. I think that helped.

I must say that the winter darkness affected everyone differently. My operations manager had to go South in November in anticipation, and I had to go in April just to see green.

Come January 6-ish, the money that the feds sent to the community for Canada Day to buy fireworks went to the Inuvik Sunrise Festival. It was great fun, although cold, and we sat in our vehicles to watch. There was hot chocolate and lots of oohs and aahs. By the way, by the time Canada Day rolled around, it was 24 hours of sun—fireworks look much better in the dark.

A truly towering Canadian

May 6, 2021

Just when I thought I had done about everything about Canada's North that might interest you, along came the news last week of the death of 88-year-old Judge Thomas Berger[6]. This man was instrumental in reminding all Canadians that there are people who need to be heard.

It has been said that Berger gave First Nations a platform to tell Canada that they wanted to have control over their ancestral lands. He certainly did a lot of his lawyering work in First Nations jurisprudence.

I remember him best for the unparalleled work he did on the Mackenzie Valley Pipeline Inquiry. When I dragged out the two-volume final report, published in 1977, all that incredible work came back to me. It was

6   thecanadianencyclopedia.ca/en/article/thomas-rodney-berger

incredibly important to our country's history and understanding of it-self[7].

The other thing that the Berger Inquiry did was give a platform to a remarkable group of young First Nations leaders. These were smart, educated, savvy people who not only saw this as an opportunity to tell their stories on a grand stage but who went on to become leaders in the formation of some remarkable forms of government.

I think of Steve Kakfwi from Fort Good Hope, who became Premier of the Northwest Territories; Nellie Cournoyea from Aklavik on the Mackenzie River Delta, who also became Premier of the Northwest Territories; Jose Amaujaq Kusugak, from the West Coast of Hudson Bay who helped drive the Eastern Arctic push to become its own territory; Ethel Blondin-Andrew, from Tulita, who was the first aboriginal woman MP in Canada; and Tagak Curley, from Salliq (Coral Harbour), who is considered a living Father of Confederation for his work leading to the creation of Nunavut.

There are others, but these are people I met as a reporter. I felt huge respect for the work that they did in a huge chunk of Canada which many in the southern part hardly knew anything about.

Some of the people here in Annapolis County may remember an Ernest Buckler event in 2019 in Bridgetown, at which one of the featured writers was my friend Whit Fraser. I am indebted to him for remembering those important days of the Berger Inquiry. He was there and I highly recommend his book *True North Rising*.

Writing columns about our North takes me back a long way, to a time in Canada that I would never have missed. I am grateful to have witnessed a major change in my country.

Travel? Yes, please!

May 27, 2021

While I miss my friends' faces and hugs a lot, I do miss travelling. I realize, as I look back now, that I have travelled all my life. I think the last time I went anywhere on a plane was in 2015. I actually had to look it up!

---

7   indigenousfoundations.arts.ubc.ca/berger_inquiry/

It started me thinking about trips I have been on over time.

I know lots of people travel all over the world on holidays. I'm not going to count those. I am going to count the ones where I moved from one place to another to live and work. Those moves were by vehicle, plane, train and ship.

We drove from Inuvik in the Northwest Territories to our place near Pincher Creek, Alberta—that's a journey of 3,681 km. We had two kittens in the vehicle with us, which made it a tad tricky finding places to stay along the way.

The other big road trip was when we moved from that place near Pincher Creek to Annapolis Royal, where we rented for almost a year before moving into our house in Centrelea. That took two vehicles and a dog, and we went 4,941 km. We visited relatives and friends along the way and I played one of my favourite CDs oodles of times: The Highwaymen—Cash, Jennings, Christopherson and Nelson. And my favourite song was 'Highwayman'. I would belt it out at the top of my lungs as I drove past the Terry Fox Memorial next to Lake Superior. And I would sing along as I drove past Rivière-du-Loup.

Back in the olden days, when my RCAF Dad was posted to the 4th ATAF base in Trier, Germany, it was quite a trip for us to get there. By ship from Montreal to Liverpool, England; by train to Chester (my birthplace) for a few months, while my Dad went on ahead to find us a place to live other than the USAF base at Bitburg. My Mom said if she was going to be in Europe, she wanted to be in Europe, not a facsimile of the US.

We got the word a month or so later and off we went—my sister and two brothers, my pregnant Mom and me. We went by train to London's Victoria Station Hotel. The next day we got on the boat train to Dover, and then the ferry to Ostend, Belgium, where we waited for the train to Luxembourg City, where Dad met us with a friend of his and drove us to Echternach, Luxembourg, where we lived over a grocery store/fish and chips place for a few months until we got a house. That trip was 950 km and we were all done in by the time we got to bed.

I miss all the lovely trips I made up North. Regina to Rankin Inlet, NU; Halifax to Inuvik, NT; Halifax to Anchorage, Alaska; Yellowknife to Igloolik and on to Nanisivik, NU; and so on. I miss my trips back to Europe to see old friends, too.

While I probably won't be going anywhere for a while, until we are allowed to go safely, I think I have at least one more trip in me.

Remembrances

November 11, 2021

There are many ways to remember the terrible events in the more recent past. One of them is to go to the Remembrance Day ceremonies around our country on November 11 each year. Another is to watch the broadcast of the ceremony that takes place in Ottawa at the Cenotaph.

That is what I do now. It keeps me out of the rain/cold/sleet for one thing, and it reminds me of going to that very spot in Ottawa with my father in the late 1940s on November 11.

As it is Remembrance Day today, I looked up the number of wars in which the Canadian territory has been involved. If one goes back to 1003 (pre-Canada, as such), apparently there was a "war" in Vinland between the Vikings and the Skraelings. "Skraelings" is what the Norse called the Indigenous people, probably in Newfoundland.

The list goes through to 2021, when the last Canadian troops came back from Afghanistan. You can see the list here:

en.wikipedia.org/wiki/List_of_wars_involving_Canada

Before Confederation, there were 15 wars fought on what is now Canadian soil; three wars were fought here after 1867. Canada's troops were involved in 20 wars around the world from 1967 to today. Two of those wars were with the United Nations troops and three were with the North Atlantic Treaty Organization.

And the number of killed and maimed? Since 1867, some 113,264 Canadians have died due to war and approximately 229,061 Canadians were wounded. I expect there were far more wounded, as those with what we now call Post Traumatic Syndrome may not have been counted, let alone diagnosed.

Some of the numbers may not seem like much when compared to the dead and injured in other countries over time. But we have to remember that, although we are big in geography, we are small in numbers. In 1867, the population of Canada was 3.4 million.

One great-uncle of mine is buried near Cambrai, France after a disastrous tank battle in World War I. A cousin of my mother's was killed in a glider accident at a training airfield in Alberta during World War II. My family has a history of men in uniform, and I am an air force brat.

It is fitting to look up the stories of some local people who went off to war. I would like to commend Lewis Falls, the publisher of *The Bridgetown Reader*, who publishes a Word Search Puzzle each week. The November 5th issue used the names of some of the military veterans from Annapolis County in the puzzle. If you look at Mr. Falls' Facebook page, he has given a brief biography of the twelve men listed.

And so we mark today as a way to remember all those who went off to war. Some were young enough to feel immortal, some were older and knew the odds, and some just didn't come home.

Christmas in Echternach

December 23, 2021

Many years ago, my family lived in the small city of Echternach in the Grand Duchy of Luxembourg, on the Sauer River on the border with Germany. My father was in the RCAF and had been posted to the NATO base at 4th ATAF (Allied Tactical Air Force) in Trier, not far away in Germany.

This time of year always brings back memories starting with Saint Nicholas Day, December 6th. The saint, dressed like a bishop, and his helper would come down the Sauer River on a barge and arrive near the bridge. There would be a procession to the town square, where the saint and his helper would stand on the steps of the Town Hall and distribute either candies or a stick, depending on how good or bad you were.

St. Nicholas Day was when children got presents. Children put their shoes out with carrots and cookies for Saint Nicholas at night and hoped for a gift in return in the morning.

And then, on Christmas Eve, everyone went to the Basilica of St. Willibrord, which had been repaired after World War II, for midnight mass. They would go home to a meal and the Christ Child brought them a gift.

The city was decorated and the windows of all the shops had lovely scenes. The patisseries were the best, with fancy cookies and candies displayed. Very tempting!

It was a magical time for our whole family. We didn't always understand what was going on in the beginning of those three years because of the language, but we soon learned. My younger siblings caught on first—kids learn language like a sponge. I ended up speaking Lëtzebuergesch...sort of. I think I got the accent right, but had to search for words.

It's an interesting language that changes depending on where you are in the country. On or near the German border, many words are Germanic, but on the French border, many words are more French. So, if I didn't know the word in Lëtzebuergesch, I would throw in a German word, if I knew it.

One of the really interesting (to me anyway) things that happened was that, about halfway through the three years we were there, I was actually thinking in the language. And I also became the interpreter for my siblings at home. Occasionally they would get really excited and move into Lëtzebuergesch and my parents couldn't quite get it. That was fun.

This little place was badly damaged during World War II. I had had no concept of what war was like when we left Canada. This city gave me a small look. Eight years after the war, there were still some piles of rubble from buildings that had been demolished. There were bullet holes in the beautiful beige stone buildings. There were stone masons repairing the cobblestoned streets.

The abbey buildings around the Basilica were being repaired. We went to school in those buildings. I learned some German, got better at French and spoke Lëtzebuergesch with my new friends.

I was always mistaken for an American, which meant I spent three years telling people about Canada. The result was a renewed love of country in me. People also loved the fact that I was a Canadian. Our country had a great reputation in Europe in those times.

I still have dear friends from Echternach whom I have kept in touch with over the decades. This little place holds a big piece of my heart and my mind. I learned about another culture, another language, another built history so much older than mine, the resilience of human beings, and the kindness of people towards a family from a faraway part of the world.

While these past many months have been a trial, I hope you all have a Happy Christmas and a Joyous New Year with your (limited number for indoor gatherings of) family and friends.

Heroes

January 27, 2022

I feel very fortunate to have met some of my heroes over time. One of them died recently—Alexa McDonough. She worked so hard in the political trenches with such honesty and tenacity that it would be hard not to give her big hoorays. I met her again a number of years ago and she was just as gracious as ever.

Her death made me think back on other people who are gone now but have left an indelible mark on my mind and soul. Here are some of them.

I was a friend of Muriel Duckworth back in the late 1960s and early 1970s. She was the leader of the Voice of Women in Halifax during those anti-Vietnam War days. I marched with her and helped wherever I could. She was dedicated beyond belief. She was kind and she could be funny. She patiently taught me what the VoW was all about.

Through that group, I met Thérèse Casgrain, a monumental intellect from Quebec. She paid for a proper berth on my train ride for a VoW conference in Calgary. She didn't want to have me sitting in coach the whole way.

And there were other heroes in that movement—the Raging Grannies, remember them?

The 4th ESTATE, as an entity, is also a hero of mine. In the late 1960s, an intrepid family started a bi-weekly, which became a weekly newspaper in Halifax. The paper attracted some of the most interesting people I have ever met. Some took a risk to write for it. Others, like me, were just lucky to be a worker bee there. That little paper caused quite a stir in the upper echelons of power of the day. It worked hard for the ordinary people—tenants of slum landlords, fishermen, artists, and more—who weren't getting recognized by the other media. There are too many to mention them all, but Nick Fillmore, the managing editor, was my hero of that time.

My great aunt Ethel, known as Auntee, was a hero of mine. She was a civil servant in Ottawa. She was the one who lived with my great-grandmother in her last years. I was told that Auntee drove her black coupe car from Ottawa to Banff to play golf either before World War II or right after. That made her a hero in a young girl's mind.

I met some remarkably strong First Nations women and men in Canada's North when I lived there. They believed that speaking in their language on the radio was one of the most important ways to help to keep the culture alive. With English being blasted from television sets from American channels, this was a daunting task.

The people who are braving the weather this winter "protecting" the forest just up off Highway 10 are my heroes. They are putting themselves out in both bad and good weather for something in which they believe strongly. That's heroic in my book.

My Mom and Dad are heroic, too. As I have said before in this column, Dad went to England to join the RAF in early 1939 and ended up flying Spitfires throughout the war. My Mom went over to England in 1940, and that's where I was born. Dad's life would have been very terrifying at times, especially since he had to parachute out of his plane in Belgium in January, 1945. He was safe, but my Mom didn't know when he would be home or if he would come home. Like so many others of that time, bravery was in large supply.

My daughters have put up with a lot of stuff in their lifetimes and they rank pretty high on the list. I'll leave the rest of my family alone for now, but you know who you are.

There are public figures who can be called heroes. There are also those who have braved hardships that we may never know about, but who need our special thoughts.

When I heard that Alexa had died, it made me think that, while we may have well-known heroes, everyday people can be heroic, too. Have a look in your memory file and think of all your heroes. We need every one of them these days.

Anne Crossman's

Nostalgic music

March 31, 2022

The other day, I heard one of my favourite pieces of music someone had posted, 'Finlandia' by Jean Sibelius. I was transported back to 1987 in Inuvik at the Sir Alexander Mackenzie School auditorium on the Mackenzie Delta of the Northwest Territories.

The Toronto Symphony on its *Canadian Odyssey* tour had come to town. The place was jam-packed. I was sitting upstairs in the balcony. The first notes started, and I wept. The tears were streaming down my face for the whole eight minutes of the piece.

I was living in the land of small trees above the Arctic Circle. I knew part of Finland was above the Arctic Circle. The beautiful music was so evocative of where I was living. I was a tad embarrassed by my behaviour, but as I look back on it now, I have much sympathy for my former self. The music still moves me.

That Toronto Symphony tour brought a wonderful friend into my life, too. The second violinist, Andrea Hansen, whose heritage was Finnish (of course!), decided then and there to start teaching fiddle music to the children of the Delta. She started a foundation called Strings Across the Sky and went North almost every year to teach.

We somehow brought (Andrea roped me in to help) the Royal Canadian Air Farce to town a few years later, and I distinctly remember hitting up everyone in the bars in Inuvik with Andrea, selling tickets. And I got to sit with Roger Abbott in the Mackenzie Hotel restaurant, giving him some bits of Inuvik lore that he could use in their skits. I must say it was kind of fun hearing what they made of my thoughts when they wowed the crowd at their performance.

I first heard Ian and Sylvia singing 'Four Strong Winds' in the 1960s while living in Eastern Canada. The song stayed with me for many years. Little did I know that I would end up living for some years just down the road from Ian's ranch in southern Alberta, many years later. The words are stuck in my brain; I can still sing that song (silently) with all the

34

words to this very day.

'Farewell to Nova Scotia' makes me think of a raucous evening at The Hoist Room in Yellowknife many evenings ago, when many former Nova Scotians (and I) hollered for the performer of the evening to sing it yet again so we could all belt it out along with him. And although it was a goodbye song, here I am back in Nova Scotia. Life is funny that way.

One early morning in Regina, a radio news guy came up to the control room where the morning show was in full swing, and handed me a piece of wire copy saying that a plane had gone down in the U.S., and it looked like Stan Rogers was on it. It took our collective breaths away.

I rushed to the record library, picked up the first Stan Rogers I could find, tore back to the studio, gave the album to the tech, told the host what was happening, and the notes of 'Fogarty's Cove' went out over the airwaves. We were absolutely silent during that wonderful song. And after the song was over, the host told our audience what had happened.

I never thought I would like Country and Western music. I got ten years of it when living in Northern Canada. But when George Jones starts on the radio singing 'He Stopped Loving Her Today', I am back in Inuvik again, knowing that one of the Lyall brothers in Cambridge Bay was a happy man listening to his favourite singer on the radio.

And the last piece I will mention is one of John Prine's—pick a song. Today, I'll pick 'Paradise'. The chorus says

> *And daddy won't you take me back to Muhlenberg County*
> *Down by the Green River where Paradise lay*
> *Well, I'm sorry my son, but you're too late in asking*
> *Mister Peabody's coal train has hauled it away*

And half of John's ashes are in that Green River.

All those memories came roaring back just because a piece of music played on the radio the other day.

A real book

May 26, 2022

I wrote a book. A real book. It has a front and back cover. It has thick, glossy pages. It has colour photos. It has words printed on the pages.

I can't believe how pleased I am about it. I wrote a book!

If you have written memories, notes on the back of old photos, stories your grandma told you over tea—consider having your own book.

A long time ago, I received my father's log books from his time in the Royal Air Force during World War II. He was a pilot and, most of his time, he flew Spitfires. My mother went to England to marry him. She kept some diaries.

As some of you know, log books can be pretty terse. So I set about finding out what I could about my parents' time during the war. I had two cousins who got into the whole project. They sent me material about the squadrons and the Spitfires as they found it. And I had lots of time to do the same.

The project grew from there. I wanted to capture the process and the research as I went along, so I started a blog. I would go along for a few weeks and then go on to another project, but that time of my parents was always in the back of my mind.

Along the way, I "met" some overseas people who knew part of the story, so an email correspondence was started. As a result, my husband and I went to Belgium to meet some of them. And then my daughter and I went over. And then my sister and I went over. Every now and then, some new bit of information would drop in my lap (or, more accurately, into my computer). And so I would add that to the blog.

A few months ago, I started having rather dreadful thoughts: what if the blog world suddenly headed out into the ether or went off to Mars or something. Horror of horrors, all that information would disappear. I had some of it at home, but not all.

This is a long way of saying that I had it all printed into a book— a real book. I took my project to Integrity Printing in Bridgetown, we designed the covers together, they printed it, sent it off to Gaspereau Press for binding and when it came back, they cut it. I had 40 copies made. It was to go to my siblings and their children. It has also gone to cousins who helped and friends across the ocean.

I have had some very kind remarks from a couple of folks of the next generation. They have asked questions which I have been happy to answer.

It should have been better edited, but when I look at it sitting on my desk with my name on the spine, my handsome Dad's portrait on the front and my Mom and Dad on their wedding day in Chester, England on the back, it makes me smile and gives me great pleasure.

I hope my mother and my Uncle Bill (who was a weekly newspaper publisher/editor) would have liked my book. Oh yes, and I sure hope Dad would have been alright with it.

Planning around a hurricane

September 29, 2022

Two years ago, I thought it might be a good idea to have a party in the summer for a significant birthday. "They" sent a plague. That stopped those plans in their tracks.

So when I heard that the plague was lessening and that anyone I was going to invite had been most careful with masking and social distancing and had been vaccinated the requisite number of times, I decided to have another go at a party. The summer was going to be too hot, we said. Flying was wretched before school started, we said. Let's try towards the end of September, we said. Surely...

People made flight and rental car bookings. Driving to Here from There needed more route planning.

And so September 24 became the date. I thought around 40 people would be here. We would have a big marquee or tent in the backyard. We would borrow real plates and cutlery from our community hall, and chairs if need be. I talked to a local caterer, and we selected a menu to accommodate everyone.

Then we started hearing that the hurricane season was starting late this year. We were down to the "E's" in tropical storms. Excellent news.

One bunch started driving on an across-the-country trip from Victoria, BC. Another flew in from Alberta. There was a flying contingent from Ontario and a driving couple from there as well.

There were lovely local friends, too.

Along came a week ago. Along came the news. Along came the emails and messages and phone calls about Hurricane Fiona.

In spite of all this, I remained optimistic. I was hellbent this party was going ahead. I said nice things to the Storm Gods of Old: Aeolus, Zeus, Set, Kymopoleia, Tempestas, Perun, Manannán mac Lir and a few other more recent deities.

And for us they held.

I am very sorry that Fiona really smacked other parts of Atlantic Canada. I do know there was lots of damage and hurt.

And so, as the news got windier and rainier, we ditched the tent idea and went to the Centrelea Community Hall.

There were close to 30 people there. There was a ton of food, with enough leftovers for the next day for the folks still around. The hall was lively, with some people getting to know other people and old friends getting together as well. And most of my family were there. The noise level was high and there was lots of laughter. What a delight!

Good things sometimes happen in times of stress as long as the strength of hope holds—not always, but sometimes.

I am very grateful for however it happened.

Christmasing across Canada

December 22, 2022

I have spent a lot of Christmases in different parts of this country and others over all these years—England, Ottawa, Trenton, Lac St. Denis (check it out online), Echternach (worth another online search), St. Hubert, Montreal, Black Point, Dartmouth, Boutilier's Point, Glen Haven, Halifax, Mahone Bay, Portugal Cove, Cross Creek, Yellowknife, Prince Rupert, La Ronge, Regina, Rankin Inlet, Inuvik, near Pincher Creek, Annapolis Royal, Centrelea and soon here in Annapolis Royal again.

Each of these places had its own way of doing things. I learned lots of different customs in different languages and cultures. Some I remember better than others because they were outside of my ordinary life.

The one thing they all had in common was good cheer. We wished each other the best of the season. We celebrated the religion or the belief of each place.

Because all of those communities are in the Northern hemisphere, we saw the dark nights get longer and some of those nights were three or four weeks long.

Our first year in Yellowknife, we drove out of town to get a tree. First, when the axe hit that frozen tree half the needles fell off with a kind of tinkling sound. Second, when we got back to the car, it wouldn't start. It was cold. After much fiddling around under the hood, we took that little tree home and dressed it up as best we could.

There were some places where we didn't have much snow and some winters that were monumentally blizzardy, with howling winds and fine driven snow that felt like it was shredding your face.

But there were usually bright lights of all the different colours and people greeting each other in the stores and in the streets with smiles, even if their scarves were pulled up over their chins.

I learned about St. Nicholas Day in Europe on December 6. And I also went to the Roman Catholic mass on Christmas Eve at the big basilica in

Echternach. It was very moving. As was going to the little Anglican Church in La Ronge on Christmas Eve. While they were far apart geographically, the sentiment from the parishioners in both places was real.

Going to my grandparents' house in Ottawa for Christmas dinner was always a treat. My grandfather had a "relationship" with a canary in a cage which was just behind him when the dining room table had all four leaves in it. He would slowly lift up his hand and run it very fast along the birdcage, sending the canary into a tizzy. While this sounds pretty bad and my grandmother had thoughts about it, too, that bird returned very quickly to the spot where his hand had been. I swear it was a game for him as well.

There were Christmases up North and a Christmas in Portugal Cove in Newfoundland. My husband had a great time cleaning ashy footprints away from the fireplace that year. And the kids made the most revolting sandwich of sardines and peanut butter, I think, for Santa. He actually took a bite. We were invited to a party where Mummers showed up, King George and some others I didn't recognize. That was fun.

And, last but not least, I would like to send my gratitude out to all my relatives and friends who sent me best wishes, love and hugs last week. It was a little overwhelming, but I would like everyone to know that your notes and stories will help give me what I need to get through this operation. I must also say that I really didn't expect the reaction. Women shared their stories. Women said they had their mammogram scheduled. Men sent lots of good wishes too.

I would like to wish everyone a good time with family and friends. Call an old friend from long ago. Wish a complete stranger Merry Christmas in the grocery store. Smile as much as you can because it will help others do the same and pass it on. We all need Good Cheer and this is mine to you.

The legacies we leave

January 12, 2023

An inordinate number of people I knew have died recently in a very short period of time—over the close of one year and the opening of a new one.

I have found myself thinking a bit differently about the death of people I knew, those whose life was cut short by some sort of sickness over which they had no control.

I have started thinking of the legacy they left behind, the legacy they created with family and friends, and with colleagues in their chosen work.

Artists of all sorts leave behind bodies of work by which we remember them. While we may not know exactly how Leonardo da Vinci was as a friend or neighbour, we certainly know what a fascinating mind he had, given the art and science information he left us.

We may not understand how Beethoven could write brilliant music which we still listen to and admire all these years later, when he was deaf.

There are five of Ian Tyson's CDs here, and when the news came along that he had died at the age of 89 (I don't think anyone would have given him that length of time), out came those terrific songs. I sang along with all of them. They reminded me of times in the past and I saw the foothills of Alberta in my mind's eye again.

While these brilliant minds have worldwide recognition and a legacy which will keep on going as long as humankind is thinking and listening and looking, our family and friends who made an impact on us while they lived are also carried on through their stories being told at gatherings.

We say things like, "Remember when we laughed 'til we cried when..." and, "That silly hat..." and, "He was so generous when..." and, "We went on that house tour and hoped we never had to live there because of the stairs..."

Those are legacies which are also carried on with photographs or home movies (remember them?) or videos taken on special occasions.

As some of us work on family genealogy, we find all kinds of bits of interesting information that others around the world have collected. Those bits are becoming part of the legacy we leave behind.

Some of us keep notes and emails and even daily journals. Those will also be part of our legacy.

While the small, everyday events and occurrences may seem trivial or unimportant or not worth much, they represent a big part of who we are and who we were.

Those little remembrances we have of other folks who are gone now are part of their stories left behind. Bring them out at family gatherings, lunches with close friends, evenings with lots of laughter and maybe even a few tears—those things are priceless.

Backyard eggs

January 26, 2023

I see that people are going into the backyard chicken business again these days. This is in the belief that they can raise chickens to lay eggs, which have begun to cost a lot of money at the grocery store.

Well, let me tell you, it's not that easy, nor is it that inexpensive.

First, you have to find out if you are allowed to raise egg-laying chickens where you live. Check with your municipality, because you can't just go out and buy the birds and put them in your backyard without permission, or common sense, for that matter.

You need a fenced-in area both to keep the chickens inside and to prevent all those varmints from getting them—think skunks, foxes, coyotes and neighbourhood dogs. Chickens like to lay eggs in some sort of shelter. There are all kinds of them: take your pick.

Then you have to get in the right feed. And then you have to get the chickens. I remember this part.

We took over a farm many years ago to look after (rent free) for various reasons (another story). There was a whole bunch of wee fluffy chicks in the upstairs back room, under lamps to keep them warm and with dishes of water and food. And they cheeped and cheeped and cheeped!

And dust! It was as if those little fluffy things had the most appalling cases of dandruff!

They eventually went outside in the spring to be free-range chickens. I am not the farmer in the family. I don't know if they laid eggs or were meat birds. I just know that while they were very cute when they were inside, I was very glad when they left the back room.

We babysat another farm after that and had chickens and ducks, for Pete's sake! I barely knew about chickens. We did get eggs. These we found in all kinds of nooks and crannies in a dilapidated barn behind the house. The kids were getting them until they found the skunk making one of her daily raids.

When it came time to move on from that farm, the kids helped to move those hens to another farm. And that's when we got a lesson in chicken hypnosis. You heard that correctly. If you pick chickens up by their feet and gently turn them upside down, they sort of go into a trance and you can take them where they need to go with much less fuss.

The kids got to keep the money from the sale of those birds. Worth every penny!

I know it's lovely to get fresh eggs, especially when you know where they came from, but I would remind you that fresh eggs make lousy hard-boiled eggs because they really don't peel very well. And you have to wipe them off to put them in that lovely bowl on the counter because they don't last as long after you wash them, so you have to refrigerate them.

Then there's the thing about the rooster who will take an immediate dislike to anyone headed his way and will fly at you, feet first, making an awful racket. If you live in a town or a city, the neighbours won't like the rooster's morning wake-up call, either.

All in all, I prefer buying my eggs at the store. I am fortunate that the price is of little concern for me, but I am also fortunate that someone else is doing all the work and keeping those hens safe from avian flu so I can have a lovely cheese omelette with D'Aubin's delicious bacon for a Friday-evening supper.

Remember the Sixties?

July 13, 2023

In the latter part of the 1960s, I was living in the Halifax area. In a recent conversation, the subject of draft dodgers came up and my mind went whistling back to those heady days.

Halifax had been a fairly sedate place in the early sixties. I always thought that the leftover grey marine paint that was used on all the Navy ships seemed to have worked its way into the city itself and its people, too.

And then the Height-Ashbury movement went swooping across the U.S. from California and eventually up to Canada, and after that it finally hit Halifax. University students wrote amazing newsletters. There were demonstrations up and down Spring Garden Road. The Voice of Women was in every one of them—I know because I was in those marches.

There were speeches on the Grand Parade in front of City Hall. There were speeches in Victoria Park. There were flyers being handed out against the Vietnam War. There was a small storefront that was run by the Marxists.

And there were the "draft dodgers". I say that in quotes because, although there was definitely a cross-border migration of young men who had received that letter from their draft board, we tended to call everyone who came across the border a 'draft dodger'.

I knew some of them. One went on to be a top-notch radio documentary producer. Another was a university professor of some renown. There were the hippies who lived in a small backwoods community in New Brunswick. As far as I know, they are still there.

There were/are hippies who lived around this part of Nova Scotia. Many enriched the area with their wish to live simply, grow their own food, build their own homes for their children, and live quietly away from the big cities. They are still here and have contributed much to those communities. They included poets and authors and artists who believed the world could be a kinder, gentler place.

When Donald Trump got elected to the presidency in the U.S. in 2016, another wave of Americans moved across the border. Should he get elected again in 2024 (that's just a year and a half away), the atmosphere will be toxic in the U.S. For all the reasons you can think of—guns, foreign policy, immigration, women's rights, religious bigotry, sexual identity—many Americans will see us as a safer place.

I see the temperate zones, both north and south, becoming more habitable places to live. Given the present climate—both meteorologically and politically—in the U.S., it wouldn't surprise me at all to see more folks moving across to a place they see as at least a bit more sane and not quite as nasty.

And so, the anger about the Vietnam War that brought Americans here in the 1960s and 1970s, has changed into a wish for a more peaceful place.

In my books, they would be welcome—just as welcome as that other group was over 50 years ago.

Why I remember

November 9 2023

For many other people, Remembrance Day is special. It is a day that means different things to different people. The following is the reason I remember.

Canadian Leader of Punjab Squadron Hit
By Denis Martin
The Royal Gazette and Colonist, Hamilton, Bermuda
Monday, February 12, 1945

WITH THE SECOND TACTICAL AIR FORCE BELGIUM, Feb. 11 (Reuters).-The leader of this celebrated "Punjab" Spitfire squadron, wounded by flak after a strafing mission of Germany, thrown out of his cockpit and baling out into the slipstream, managed to drift back into the Allied lines and land on the doorstep of his favourite "pub" (tavern).

He is Squadron Leader P.V.K. Tripe, Distinguished Flying Cross, of 328 James Street, Ottawa, and he is now on his way back to Canada.

The mission had yielded about five motor transport and one tank when Tripe's aircraft was hit and the mainplane ripped open. Five pieces of shrapnel lodged in his right arm. Tripe nursed the aircraft towards the Allied lines when a heavy explosion on the starboard side stripped the fuselage and wing. Tripe stood up in the cockpit and let the slipstream whip him into the air as the Spitfire turned into the death roll. Landing by parachute near a wood, Tripe recognized that he was almost on top of a roadhouse only a few miles from the aerodrome. Pilots of the Spitfire wing had held a nightly rendezvous at the inn for some weeks and the patron gave Tripe an enthusiastic reception.

"Nice of you to come so early" he shouted but when he saw that Tripe was wounded, he brought out a bottle of his best cognac—not the stuff sold over the bar—and called up an army truck. Tripe has completed over 1,200 flying hours and left for Canada after a brief stay in hospital.

You see, Squadron Leader P.V.K. Tripe, Distinguished Flying Cross, of 328 James Street, Ottawa was my Dad. I am ever so grateful that he came home after World War II. Many fathers didn't.

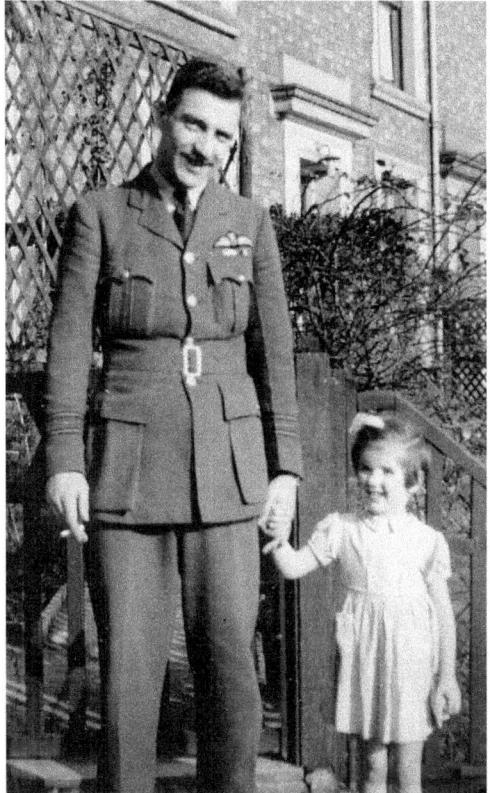

My Dad and me
Chester, England, 1944.

Anne Crossman's

Politics

Watching what goes on politically locally, provincially, nationally and occasionally internationally has been interesting to me ever since I was able to vote. I have made it a point to know what is happening in those places which might have some effect on where I am living.

I have lived in almost every province and territory in Canada. Each place had its own set of issues which became part of my research on how I would vote. I have been very interested in who was brave enough to put their name forward to run in an election.

I had always said that I would run one day, and eventually I did. My daughter was my campaign manager—she kept me going when I really just wanted another cup of coffee.

When the votes were counted, I didn't win, but I wasn't at the bottom of the heap.

People who came to the house on election night were sad and kept saying things like, "You should have won!" and, "I can't believe you didn't win!"

I was just fine. I had done what I said I would do, and met some really nice people, including the guy who beat me.

Anne Crossman's

Politics: theirs and ours

November 19, 2020

It has been an amazing four years for us political junkies.

I've been a junkie since the first time I voted for John Turner in Montreal, many, many years ago. I was sooo much younger then. I may have voted for him because he was very handsome. I have totally forgotten what the issues were, but it was very twitchy being an Anglo in Montreal in 1962, I can tell you.

As the years went by, I voted in every election that was going at the time—municipal, provincial and federal. I tried to pay attention to the issues, the candidates and the parties.

Since the Elephant below us[8] influences a lot of what happens politically and economically up here, it's been hard not to pay attention to the outrageous behaviour of their leadership. The phrase that comes around and around is "It can't get any worse"—and then it does. And it's been getting worse every day for four years.

On the US Election Night, 2020, I had three bags of Election Chips to get me through until I fell asleep. I polished one off.

The next morning I learned that Miss Vicki's had recalled some of her chips. Fortunately, the ones I had were okay, because I needed the last two bags to get me through Day 2. And then there was Day 3.

Will That Man[9] ever give up and move out?

And we have been having elections all over the place up here—New Brunswick, British Columbia and Saskatchewan, to start with. Each of those produced a lot more of the same.

And, not to be left out, we have had municipal elections in Nova Scotia. Quite a few changes have happened here. There is the first woman mayor of Cape Breton Regional Municipality, and there's the second woman

---

8   Pierre Trudeau, 1969: "Living next to [the United States] is in some ways like sleeping with an elephant. No matter how friendly and even-tempered the beast, one is affected by every twitch and grunt."

9   U.S. President Donald Trump.

mayor in Annapolis Royal.

Annapolis County Council has five incumbents, five new councillors, and one almost new. There is a new Warden, Alan Parish, and a new Deputy Warden, Mike Gunn. Mr. Parish is new to council and Mr. Gunn has been on council for at least one term.

Since I live and voted in Annapolis County, I will be paying attention to how this new council works. There has been a lot of heat here in the past months. There are issues to discuss, there are wounds to be healed and a way to be found to go forward.

I may be one of the few who watch council video meetings online the day after they take place. Since both Annapolis Royal and Middleton put their meetings live on Facebook, I think it would be useful for the County to do the same. I hope all the people (who will still be doing Zoom meetings, by the way[10]) are able to be reasonable and accountable.

PS – I just watched the first meeting (Thursday, November 12, 2020) of Annapolis County's Committee of the Whole, done via Zoom. Hang on for a very rocky road ahead, my fellow County residents.

Our neighbour to the south

January 21, 2021

I have a many-pictured view of the US, America, our neighbour to the south.

There was the time when my best friend's cousins came to stay and we would play Monopoly for almost their whole visit to Ottawa in the summers of the late 1940s. They were always a little more "something" than we were, even then.

There was the odd attitude that I saw when living in Luxembourg in the 1950s, not that long after World War II, when I saw the double-edged side of the feelings towards the Americans in Europe. The local people liked the Coca Cola, the swagger, the dollars, the music, Hollywood, the

---

10   Under COVID health protection provisions.

jeans. What they didn't like was the feeling of being given charity, feeling beholden, the brashness, the emigration of their young women as US wives.

Around that time, I believe that "real" jeans were being sold on the black market in Russia. When I was there, people thought I was American when they first met me. As soon as I said I was Canadian, the attitude brightened up considerably. I think I educated a whole bunch of people about my country in three years.

And then there was the innocent admiration of the Kennedys in the 1960s, the Camelot-like vision the US networks sent us on our TV screens. And the money, Hollywood, music, the flower children. And the horrible tragedy of the assassinations, Vietnam, demonstrations, the Chicago riots, the Detroit riots, Watts riots.

The 1970s saw us glued to the world of business. There was still Hollywood and the music.

And then my attention wavered and I stayed in my own country for quite a while, looking after me and mine.

But the US was always there—large and complex, rich and poor, multicoloured and the huge melting pot.

And we were there for the US during the horror of 9/11. Many remember the planes landing and parking in Gander. I remember all the planes that landed and parked in Halifax and the people who opened up their homes to take those passengers in.

I was just as horrified at the riots and the racial battles of the past in that country as I was a couple of weeks ago at the spectacle of those people storming through the Capitol Building in Washington. I was horrified at a man who had such a mittful of power, wielding that power for battle amongst his own people.

And the big question is, how did they get to that point? How did this man get to sit behind that *Resolute* desk? He was such a "different" and "unlikely" person to become president. He was outrageous, flamboyant and courted the media mercilessly. They gave in. How could they resist? I won't go through all the stunts—we know them well. He appealed to the basest of us. I say "us" advisedly. It was so hard to look away from the swirl and the outlandish. He kind of took over the world.

And so we come the sad day, January 6, 2021 . An attention-demanding infantile figure in the law-making hall of the US with horns and tattoos. A young woman who believed in the QAnon fantasies is dead. A police officer dead from injuries sustained in the building. Three others dead from who-knows-what. Papers strewn about, No respect for the building's history or significance.

And the world watched in wonder. The "enemies" of the US laughed, no longer behind their hands. The "enemies" said, "We hardly had to do anything and it worked." The place was in disarray. Some of the elected officials were finally ashamed at what they had done and what they had made possible.

And the media personalities tut-tutted and said they were trying to tell us about this all along. They had done their fact-checking. They had called out the lies. They had cried out warnings. Or they had tut-tutted about those "commies" à la Joseph McCarthy and praised the man who had done such wonderful things for the stock market.

And now, every day there is something new to watch—another impeachment, a sob-story from that man which wouldn't convince a kid, charges being laid, and an inauguration.

And here we are—watching over the fence as this big American cousin tries to right its ship of state, make its way to a better path, heal its friends and neighbours and show the world that all is not lost.

Grumpiness!

June 24, 2021

There used to be four major issues facing Annapolis County Council: garbage, internet, Gordonstoun School[11] and communications. Now there are five: garbage, internet, Gordonstoun, Basinview Centre and communications.

The garbage issue has been put in abeyance for a year, but it will be rearing its ugly head, no doubt. People are still anxious to get internet connectivity quickly and of a quality equal to what the big cities get. The school seems to be in jeopardy. The Basinview Centre looks like it will be erased from our memories. And we still don't have anyone in charge of communications since Larry Powell's contract was not renewed.

---

11   This was a proposal to create a branch of Scotland's Gordonstoun School on the site of the former Upper Clements theme park.

The old Britex building seems to have been sold (tax sale bid) for a song—$15,100—and I haven't heard what will be going on there other than further vandalism by "the lads" (as Deputy Warden Michael Gunn put it some time ago).

I am trying very hard to think of something positive to say, something going forward, something to cheer about, something to get behind and see to the end. If I come up with anything, before I finish writing this column, I'll be sure to put it in.

There are folks still angry about the trees being stripped away in our county. There are folks still very angry about that dump site on the Arlington Road.

Back at the turn of the last century, our county used to be a bustling place with lots of commercial activity going on. There was ship building, shipping, farming, cider operations, barrel making, regular trade with New Brunswick, etc., etc. Look at us now. Quite frankly, I find us quite pathetic.

About the only thing that is moving rapidly is the sale of various parcels of real estate. There are people who think we have something here. They like the scenery, they like the history and the heritage. They like the people. And, of course, they like the prices of the properties.

I do realize that I'm a tad grumpy, but I think we need to see something positive happening from our local elected officials, especially in this Time of COVID.

PS – I attended a wonderful gathering of great friends last weekend. We haven't been together for months and months and months. We laughed like mad over silly things and it was delightful!

PPS – All my friends are getting vaccinated, or are vaccinated already. Hooray!

Canadians must be vigilant

June 30, 2022

Not to be overly dramatic, but I am as angry, perplexed, and worried this week as I was when I awoke in the middle of the night on November 7, 2016 to learn that Donald Trump had won the presidential election in the United States of America.

The US is huge; not as big in population as some other countries, but huge in worldly influence. It is rich in wealth, in innovation, in science and space. It has been a young, vigorous entity in the world. It was naïve sometimes, but we forgave some of those gentle little quirks as being kind of charming.

But there is now a dark cloud spreading across that map. The cloud is called by many names: bigotry, racism, small-mindedness, uneducated, meanness, right wing philosophy, religious zeal, my-way-or-you're-dead, gun-toting, lying political swamp, and fear—lots of fear.

And you might ask, "Why should you care about what happens in another country?"

That's a very good question.

The answer is, "Because we are surrounded by it—below, to the northwest and the far west."

We share a defence system. Think of the recent announcement that NORAD will be beefed up again across the Canadian Arctic.

And after Trump, there was the assault on the US Capitol on January 6, 2021 and now there is this US Supreme Court overturning of the 1973 Roe vs. Wade decision that women had the constitutional right to seek an abortion. I do remember when that decision was made.

Why should we care here in Canada? Because there are bits and pieces of that dark cloud seeping into this country.

I remember hearing of some of the horrors that went on before Roe vs. Wade was approved. I know some of what happened in this country, when there was no safe way to have an abortion. The infections that made a woman sterile. The deaths that resulted from the so-called "back-room" abortions.

There are as many reasons to end a pregnancy as there are women in the world. Each and every one must have the right—not the privilege—to make that decision herself. Some may choose not to for various reasons. That is also their right.

We must be vigilant in our country to preserve these rights.

I love elections!

July 22, 2021

As I have said many times before, I am a news junkie, and I am also a die-hard election junkie. I will be following as much information as I can get during this Nova Scotia election scheduled for Tuesday, August 17.

I have voted in every election (federal, provincial and municipal) that I have been able to since I turned 21. That's a lot of elections. I have worked on a few campaigns over time, and I have worked for Elections Nova Scotia and for a couple of municipal elections. I even ran once—quite a few years ago.

Let me tell you, elections demand hard work. Candidates work hard getting their message out there, doing the door knocking (with a mask this time out, I expect), holding rallies (can't kiss babies these days but I imagine there will be sore elbows from all that bumping), making sure your team is doing its work and that the money is being properly handled, lots of phone calls and lots of emails. The very thought of all that makes me weary. You have to be very, very dedicated to want to be an elected person.

The worker bees in the campaign offices burn the midnight oil getting those signs out, making phone calls, arranging for those rallies to run smoothly, watching the money and holding the candidate's hand when they falter from fatigue and wonder why the heck, they agreed to do this.

The folks who run the elections in those offices in each constituency are heading off for training in Halifax. They will find out what latest technology is being used, how to log every vote, how to solve problems, how to deal with the paperwork and mail-in ballots, what to do with an inmate who wants to vote, how to get a new elector registered and how to manage all those VICs (Voter Information Cards, usually yellow).

And then there are the issues. You can bet your bottom dollar that each voter has their own hobby horse. While there may be general agreement on some of the big issues here in Nova Scotia— not enough family doctors, roads, jobs, roads, jobs, environment, jobs—each person would like something entirely different. These other issues may not even be ones that the provincial government is responsible for.

That doesn't seem to matter. The cries will be heard. And with the internet and Facebook these days, we will hear them all. And we will hear the nasties and the uglies and the libellous and the slanderous and the ignorant.

I hope that every eligible voter is voting this time. We disgrace the name of democracy if we don't vote. And then the old saying "you get the government you deserve" becomes real.

By the way, I would like to recommend three books by Graham Steele about politics in general and Nova Scotia politics in particular: *What I Learned About Politics*, *The Effective Citizen* and *Nova Scotia Politics: 1945-2020*. Mr. Steele has a good head on his shoulders and writes in a very readable way.

What follows an election

August 26 2021

So I wrote a column that was to go in last week's *Annapolis Valley Register,* two days after the Nova Scotia election. I thought it was pretty good. It was responsible and gave good advice and so on.

And then the election happened. I called it wrong. I wasn't the only one. I really thought it was going to be close, with the Liberals in a minority position. As the time drew closer to Election Day, I wavered— just not as far as the electorate, though. The voters gave the victory, and a majority government, to the Progressive Conservative Party.

One of my favourite political writers is Graham Steele. I think he called it. Nova Scotia's electorate really gets kind of fed up with whatever party is in power after a while. And they go to the polls saying, "It's time for a change."

Back to the "ghost" column, which will remain on my hard drive in its former form, I am resurrecting part of it for you today:

> Here we are Post-Election Day Number One. What can we do to ensure that the reconstituted Nova Scotia government does what the candidates said they were going to do, now that they made it into our legislature?
>
> I don't believe it is naïve to hold politicians to their promises. If war breaks out, if the pandemic morphs again into something worse, if the world economy goes down the drain or some other catastrophic event happens, then the new government can be excused from not doing some of the things they said they were going to do.
>
> Otherwise, they must be held to account. It is up to us—the people who voted them in—to pay attention to what was promised.

Here is what Premier-designate Tim Houston said on his website during the campaign:

> We can put Nova Scotians on a path to financial sustainability and ensure that we fix the issues in healthcare, mental health, and seniors' care.
>
> We can support our traditional industries and build an environment plan that fights climate change.
>
> We can make our province a magnet for doctors, investors, students and tourists alike, and remain proud of our traditions and our heritage.

The Progressive Conservatives have four years to accomplish what they promised. They may not get it all done, but we should pay attention.

One thing I'd like to add: the Nova Scotia Progressive Conservative Party is not the Conservative Party of Canada, nor is it the United Conservative Party of Alberta, and it isn't the Progressive Conservative Party of Ontario. Tim Houston is not a Doug Ford, or a Jason Kenney or an Erin O'Toole. He is a "red" Tory.

It is up to us to keep informed of the actions that come from the prom-
ises. Read those government news releases on the provincial government website, pay attention to the media—they cover a lot of this stuff.
Keep in touch with your MLA and her/his office. Ask questions. Be polite.
Don't rant, either on the phone or on social media. It doesn't get you anywhere. Let your MLA know about stuff that goes right for you, too. Sometimes good things happen.

Consider this part of your job as a citizen of Nova Scotia. You really do
have an obligation to our civil society.

Think, then vote

September 2, 2021

Having just gone through a provincial election in which we had an even
lower voter turnout than in previous years, I am worried. As I understand it, there was a turnout of just over half the registered voters.

Votes cast:	422,758
Valid votes:	421,051 (99.6%)
Rejected votes:	1,612 (0.4%)
Declined votes:	95 (0.0%)
Registered electors:	759,341
Voter turnout percentage:	55.67%[12]

I find that rather shocking. It shouldn't matter that the election was held
in the summer months. I have badgered people to vote—you choose, but
vote. I have said this before. And now we have another election coming.

As I watch my television and see all those people in Afghanistan trying
to get out of their home country and get to someplace else because they
feel they are not safe in the place where they were born, I am reminded
about the privilege and rights we have living in our own country. I ima-

---

12   Statistics from Elections Nova Scotia

gine packing up what is absolutely necessary in a small bag, grabbing my spouse and my children and running a gauntlet of armed men to get to the airport, and hoping like hell we can get on a plane to anywhere else. Given my age, I wouldn't make it.

I think of those who sit in their homes, afraid to go on the street to buy groceries or other essentials because they don't have the proper paperwork to show to whomever wants to see it for whatever reason.

I can't imagine what that is like.

This is my wish for my fellow Nova Scotians: think of what I have described, and think about the improvements or the changes you'd like to see in our federal government system. Think about some of the issues you have talked to your neighbour, your spouse, your siblings or your best friends about. See which of your local candidates, or which political party or its leader speaks to your idea of what change should be made, and vote.

There are some important issues to look at:

- our health care system—throwing money at its problems may not be the only or the best fix
- the climate crisis—again, throwing money at projects may not be the only or the best fix
- child care
- Truth and Reconciliation Commission Calls to Action
- long term care facilities
- quality of leadership
- the COVID pandemic
- the state of our military leadership
- First Nations' fishery rights

There are more, and you certainly have your own important issues to consider.

There was a time when families always voted for one party. The "tradition" went down through the descendants, so if your great grandfather voted Tory, you did, too. I suspect and hope those days are mostly over.

This is me being a nag again: think, then vote.

What a bunch!

September 8, 2022

What a place we live in! Is anyone else ashamed of our local government? It really is hard to know what to say. There are some words and thoughts that are probably litigious so, given that our warden is/was a media lawyer, I'll skip those.

How on earth did that hiring committee come up with David Dick to fill the role of Chief Administrative Officer for Annapolis County? I have no idea what he did to finally bring the majority of the County Council to decide to cancel his five-year contract 15 months in. We will probably hear at some point—given the local grapevine.

My main concern at this time is the staff in that Annapolis County building in Annapolis Royal. What must they be going through with all this turmoil rolling through the halls.

The end of the last County Council was bad enough. And what went on during that election campaign was horrendous. The behaviour of some was quite dreadful and totally unnecessary.

I imagine we'll hear soon about another court case or possibly even two.

This does not reflect well on us as voters. How did we elect this bunch!

When the next hiring committee is struck, there might be a bit more "due diligence" done. I do hope that a new group is chosen. I also wonder how many applicants the council is likely to get, given our present reputation.

I saw that the warden was quoted in one news story as saying, "Change can be difficult. However, Council is committed to moving forward to ensure the excellent services our residents have come to expect are maintained."

What an empty remark! Change—two Chief Administrative Officers in just over 2 years and both "let go" in a hard action—sure is some kind of change.

So my fellow (approximately) 16,000 eligible voters (as of the 2021 StatsCan census), start leaning on those elected folks in the newly renovated brick building in Annapolis Royal to make them accountable and their decisions and actions transparent. Weren't those the words whipping through the air before the November 2020 municipal election? I'm pretty sure that's what I heard.

Annapolis County municipal government must be the laughing stock of the province at this time.

As my grandmother used to say, "What a bunch!"

It is important to vote

September 9, 2021

The federal Tory platform book which Erin O'Toole is waving about reads like a left-of-centre platform. It would seem that he is trying to woo those Liberals who don't like the current Prime Minister and might like to have a looky-loo at the Tories.

The problem with that is...O'Toole's party. If he gets in as Prime Minister, forms a cabinet, and starts trying to get the planks of that platform put in place, his party will eat him for lunch!

We have to remember who is in this Tory party. It is made up of

- The red Tories (fewer and farther between these days)
- The "progressive" Tories (also hard to find and not too different from the red ones)
- The business/capitalist folks
- The "economy is everything" people
- The "freedom to do whatever I want" folks who may be anti-vaxxers, "guns are my right", anti-abortionists, and climate change deniers

- And the downright "Holy-Mackerel" types.

Can you imagine having to get all this lot moving in one direction?

On the other hand, O'Toole and his campaign managers may be deliberately trying to be sorta-Liberal in order to suck votes from the Liberals and even the NDP. But then one still has the problem of what to do if he gets in.

And let's have a look at the Liberals. There are some doubting Thomases out there. They may like the middle-of-the-road of the Liberal party itself, but they aren't too keen on the leader for a number of reasons, it seems. He doesn't always feel sincere. Even though I still think his government handled the COVID-19 business pretty well, given the complexity of it all, I'm not sure he can get enough votes on that alone. The gun issue may be what sorts the wheat from the chaff.

The NDP with Jagmeet Singh seems to be rolling along. He has loosened up somewhat, can deliver some good, straight-forward comments. And the Greens may lose some votes to the NDP because of the kerfuffle within their office.

Once again, it is important to vote. Around ten countries in the world have mandatory voting with a few provisos like making it is voluntary if you are over 70; and in some places enforcement is a bit slack.

Australia brought in legislation in 1924, and if you can't provide a good excuse for not voting, you can be fined AU$20 to AU$50 (CAD$18 to CAD$46).

Some countries are pretty strict. Samoa will issue fines.

In Singapore, "the non-voter is removed from the voter register until he/she reapplies and provides a reason. Fine applies only if the voter does not have valid reason for not voting. The non-voter is also disqualified from being a candidate at any subsequent Presidential or Parliamentary election."[13]

While I doubt "mandatory" voting would happen here, there are some countries that believe it is worth having.

Autumn comes on Wednesday, September 22, 2021, two days after the federal election, and brings the "Season of mists and mellow fruitfulness", as Keats says.

Misty it may be, I'm doubtful about that "mellow" part, though.

---

13   Information from the International Institute for Democracy and Electoral Assistance website. Canada is a member.

What politicians say matters

September 30, 2021

The Deputy Warden, Michael J. Gunn of District 8—which includes the community of Bear River, which is just across the river from the Bear River First Nation—was the only councillor who voted last week against the motion to have September 30 declared a paid holiday for county employees to commemorate the Truth and Reconciliation Day, as declared by most of the government bodies across Canada.

He did not give a reason for voting against this action. His question to staff was, "How many paid holidays do staff get now?" Then he voted against having this one.

This, gentle readers, is the Deputy Warden of the Municipality of the County of Annapolis in 2021. This is after the terrible findings of the residential schools' unmarked cemeteries. When the rest of our country wants to try to make some kind of amends the best way it knows how, this man votes against having a paid holiday to honour those little kids taken from their homes—especially those who never came home again.

I can't really say whether he is totally heartless about the day of memorials or if he just can't bear to give the hard-working staff of the county a day off with pay. Either way, it is reprehensible.

Second, the Deputy Warden, also voted against a motion to have staff and council vaccinated against COVID-19 by a particular date. He told council that he knew of more people who had had adverse effects from the vaccine—which he said wasn't really a vaccine—than people who had had the sickness. He said that one side effect was someone who got blood clots. He only knew of one person who got the disease, and that was "someone who travelled back from the Middle East, from an oil project."

During the discussion about the vaccination motion, it was pointed out that the N.S. Association of Municipal Administrators have been working on a template which municipalities can use to get their own policy in place. Other councillors asked a number of reasonable clarification questions. Gunn waited until the end of the discussion to bring forward his remarks.

It leaves me breathless that we have someone on our county council who does not seem to believe in science and calls into question whether the vaccine is worth it because it can be dangerous. He didn't seem to care that this policy was intended to protect the people who work for us at the county offices. It makes one wonder if we will hear how many councillors have received the first two vaccine shots to protect themselves and their families, friends and colleagues?

What politicians say matters—no matter if it's local, provincial or federal politics. They can influence public opinion. And just because this was at the local level doesn't mean it's not dangerous. Both Alberta and Saskatchewan are examples of the damage politicians can make with their words.

I can tell you that I am also very disappointed in the rest of the council for not calling Gunn out on these two items. Someone in that meeting should have said something.

Crickets!

Voting age

December 16, 2021

Discussion over a nice collection of snacking tidbits the other evening moved from subject to subject, as it does when a group of friends get together.

We covered quite a lot of ground, from the clear-cutting dispute to provincial politics to federal politics and what was new in each of our families—you know, the usual comfortable chit-chat amongst people who are hardly ever surprised by the topics.

Then one person said he really believed that those young people who have banded together to lobby for lowering the voting were absolutely right. He was quite firm. How low would they like the voting age to go? From 18 to 16 was the answer.

And we older folks around the table—some older than others, mind—

said the young are the ones going to have to deal with climate change and with some changes in our political system—changes in attitudes in the political parties, new parties, even the demise of some parties.

These young people have instant access to information that we didn't have when we were 16, or even 18, for that matter. Young people who think about issues have non-traditional, digital libraries to do research in like no other person before them. They will need to be careful with the digital world and verify the sources of what they take in. They will have the ability to try new technologies to turn back the erosion, calm the heat waves and the droughts and the flooding from the skies.

My example might be the same as that of many others of my age. Back then, I had some sense of what was going on in the world, but didn't dwell on those issues. I had opinions (that never changed) but they were probably fairly poorly-informed ones. I do strongly remember that, when I turned 21, I could vote. That was important to my parents, and they handed that conviction down to me.

I have heard young people discussing big issues, and having all that vigour and passion for the things they feel strongly about. They are well-spoken and are well-informed.

And they will be the same as older citizens who are interested in how things get done, in how they are governed, and in how things should be changed. Those are the people who vote because they understand it makes a difference—a big difference.

This younger generation will make their share of mistakes, but they must be given a seat at the governing table. It will be a way for this country to start looking to the future with fresh new eyes and a lot of vigour. And they must be far-sighted, as they have the greatest stake in that future.

Governments and their behaviours

October 27, 2022

While I realize the summer is a time when things, especially news, are slow, I have no idea how I missed this tidbit of information: the Canada

Foreign Buyer Ban. I'm pretty sure it would have registered because I believe this Bill C-19—the Budget Implementation Act, 2022 which was given Royal Assent on June 23—happened around the time the Houston government was talking about the tax on part-time homeowners in Nova Scotia.

So that was then, this is now. Here is the gist: "Canada will ban foreign nationals from buying homes starting January 2023—with notable exemptions for permanent residents and temporary residents, including temporary workers and international students."[14] The ban is for two years.

This measure is supposed to cool the housing market. It will prevent foreign buyers using the Canadian housing market as a bank—a place to park their money. These places often stay empty for long periods of time until the owner needs that money for some other investment.

I guess extreme times require extreme measures. We'll see how this measure works out.

Speaking of the federal government, remember way back during the last federal election campaign there was lots of talk about a national pharmacare plan? I haven't heard anything lately on that one. Back in May of this year, over 1,000 "health professionals and experts" wrote to the federal government saying that the pace and scope of the proposed act for 2023 need to be brought forward quickly after that major 2019 report from the advisory council.

The feds yet again: although the Phoenix compensation program expired in March 2020, I understand there are still federal government employees who have not had their pay cheques cleared up. That "system" either paid people too much or didn't pay them what they were owed.

And let's move on to the CRTC. What a bunch! The situation with cell phone service in this country is really awful. I understand we pay the highest fees for service in the G7 countries, or even in more countries than that. And then we had that recent big outage by Rogers, who are now running some of the most cloying TV ads I've seen in a long time saying how they are just going to be fantastic in the future. And now the recent Fiona fiasco, with cell phone towers' generators not working so no one could call 911 or anyone else for days. And the CRTC is studying the situation.

That's it for the federal government. I'll skip the provincial government this week, although there is something to be said about that

---

14   Department of Finance news release.

Speaker "problem". Why on earth do we need a Speaker and five Deputy Speakers here in Nova Scotia? I'm pretty sure that's what I read.

On to the closest of governments, the Municipal Council of the County of Annapolis. There will be a special election this fall for the District 3 council seat presently held by Alan Parish, as he is resigning his seat and therefore his wardenship. I will be paying attention over the next few months even though I will be out of the district and in Annapolis Royal by then.

Elections are always fascinating to watch. The rumour mill is gearing up to see who will be running. There might be quite a few wanting that job.

Changing of the guard

November 24, 2022

There is a change at the top of the Annapolis County municipal government. The new warden is Alex Morrison, a seasoned manager for many years and one who understands Roberts Rules of Order and how this part of Nova Scotia works. Warden Morrison also has international experience, given his time as manager of the sadly-gone Pearson Peacekeeping Centre. His resume is well worth looking up.

He is joined by Deputy Warden Brad Redden, who has paid close attention to the governance of the county over the past two years. He has made some thoughtful remarks on many subjects. There is also an interim Chief Administrative Officer at this time, Doug Patterson.

There will be a special election on January 28 for District 3 to replace Alan Parish, who resigned as warden and as counsellor. No word yet on who will be running.

I trust this new regime is a positive, forward-looking step for the county. And I wish them well.

In other news, I think there's a new group of back-to-the-landers in these parts. They are young families who are buying rural properties with a view to do subsistence farming and raising their children in a rural environment.

I believe this is a good thing. First, it lowers the median age of this area. Second, it injects some new ideas and new enthusiasm and, let's face it, younger, stronger residents.

I find I am wearing my mask more often these days. I saw Dr. Strang[15] on television last week urging us to do so. He got us through the really rough part of this COVID business, so I'm prepared to listen to him again. I have had all five COVID shots, plus the flu shot. But I am not taking any chances.

And to end off this week, we have moved into Annapolis Royal. This is a big change for us, but, as someone pointed out, we are four doors down from the place we rented back in 1998. The convenience is amazing. On one side of us is Legal Aid. And on the other side is the hardware store, the liquor store and the funeral home. And across the street are not one but two grocery stores. The home of the ambulance is also across the street. I would say we are covered.

Those Mounties!

April 6, 2023

When I was about seven years old and living in Ottawa, my very best girl-friend lived across the street. She had older siblings—one sister worked for the Department of Indian and Northern Affairs, the other sister was married, and her older brother was a Mountie. No surprise, I guess, because her father was a Mountie as well.

I remember going down the back stairs to their kitchen one afternoon and there were father and son in their red serge. Oh my, they were so handsome and glamorous. I even believe the son was a member of the famed Musical Ride.

I say all this because, as for many Canadians, for me the RCMP represented Canada. They are known all over the world. They give horses to the monarch. They rode in the cortège for Queen Elizabeth's funeral.

And as I sat here last Thursday listening to sirens going by to the old

---

15   Nova Scotia's Chief Medical Officer of Health

Upper Clements Park[16] and watched the release of the Mass Casualty Commission's joint public inquiry report into Canada's worst mass shooting[17], I wondered where the respect for those Mounties went.

While the latest assault on Upper Clements Park structures is tragic, it is not nearly in the same category as what went on in Portapique and area. But these two events are now linked for me.

The inquiry laid blame on the Mounties. The two parts that I heard right away were the lack of communications both during that rampage and after. You will, no doubt, have read or heard all the details by now.

There is lots of blame to go around for the vandalism at the park. I am not going through the torturous journey about the ownership and who was responsible for what in that department. But, where were the Mounties when all the vandalism was taking place? They are the police force looking after Annapolis County. Did anyone call them? Surely, they did. And surely someone knows who did all the destruction there. Were they someone's teenage kids? Were they adults ripping and tearing to get something to sell to someone?

I don't know what the answer is to all my questions. What I do know is that rural Canada is not very well policed. The whole policing structure needs to be overhauled. Rural municipalities can't afford their own police forces. Smaller towns can, just barely. Big cities can. But the boonies have had to put up with something that isn't working.

In the Mass Casualty Commission's Executive Summary and Recommendations, the Commissioners say

> Rural community well-being is constrained by limited access to services, poverty, and under-inclusion, and in some cases, this negatively affects the occupational health and safety of rural service providers. Urban bias in policy-making and service delivery contributes to inadequate public infrastructure and services in rural communities.

Their Recommendation C.1 says

---

16 On March 30, 2023, arsonists destroyed a stone heritage building, the former Prescesky House, which had been part of Upper Clements Park's attractions.

17 On April 22-23, 2020, Gabriel Wortman killed 22 people and set fires in sixteen locations in north and central Nova Scotia. On March 30, 2023, the Mass Casualty Commission issued its final report, which was highly critical of the RCMP.

that a) Provincial and territorial governments should take steps to address urban bias in decision-making by fostering meaningful inclusion of rural communities in all areas affecting them. And b) the federal government should support the inclusion of rural communities in decision-making on issues within their jurisdiction.

I am sorry to see the image of the Mounties being dragged through the mud, but until a major change happens at the top and the whole force gets on board, I have no doubt that the vandalism here in rural Nova Scotia will continue, with no one paying the price.

A mess in Windsor

April 27, 2023

Okay, enough is enough!

Whoever is responsible for the death trap on Highway 101 where it passes Windsor had better start doing something before there is an actual death! The original idea for twinning the Highway 101 causeway, which backed the water up from the Avon River to make a lake, has been fraught with problems. The lane closures, no yellow markings, sudden concrete barriers which change by the weeks and months are very dangerous. Why there hasn't been a death by now is a total mystery! Driving home from Halifax at night a week or so ago was a terror.

I would like to declare the federal Department of Fisheries and Oceans (DFO) an absolute disaster area. Apparently, this is the place where most of the blame lies[18]. But there is a lot of blame to go around here.

---

18 Darren Porter, a fisher and researcher in the Windsor area, sent a response to this column: "It is not DFO's fault this project went sideways in Sept 2018, when the province left the evidence-based approach for the decision-based, evidence-manufacturing approach in an attempt to save the lake. The province ignored its expert panel and chose to go with politics."

And why on earth did Nova Scotia Public Works start ripping and tearing up the highway before they got the go-ahead from DFO? Answer me that one!

This is the Public Works department which is now saying that they have their act together and are almost ready to send off the final information to DFO and everything should be hunky-dory and finished up by the end of the 2025-2026 construction season! Are you kidding me—2025-2026?

Why is the mayor of Windsor not sitting in Premier Tim Houston's office night and day begging, pleading, harrying and being downright nasty about this?

The complaints started with the pumpkin race people. Then there were the farmers upstream. Then there were the fishers. And all those folks who expected the "lake" to remain forever—built houses overlooking that nice little body of water—are mighty angry now, too.

I may have missed any comments by the PC Party's MLA for the Windsor area, Melissa Sheehy-Richard. I wonder if she has been asking her compadres in the hallways of the legislature, "Hey, how's it going with the highway project in my constituency?"

And who is the MP for this riding? Why, it's Kody Blois (Liberal), who is quoted as saying that he will be leaning on his government to see that the provincial government's submission to DFO is dealt with expeditiously—which is on its way, apparently. I wonder where he has been, if he's just now going to be leaning on one of his government's departments.

So the new provincial Department of Communities, Culture, Tourism and Heritage is busy working on their 2023 tourism campaign. How's that going, folks? Have any of you driven down Highway 101 past Windsor lately to see Grand Pré, or the Michelin plant where the new exit is going so it will be better for local folks dealing with those terrible big trucks?

And I suppose that same Department of Tourism will be mentioning Fort Anne, and Digby scallops, and the Wharf Rat Rally, and Brier Island and all the other terrific places for tourists to see in those TV ads and in the online *Doers & Dreamers Travel Guide*. And, of course, there's the wineries. And Acadia University in Wolfville, along with the theatre there.

Good luck, tourists! We love you and we want to you to have a good time. Oh, and by the way, watch out for the deadly construction zone as you go by Windsor. We wouldn't want to lose you.

PS: I sure hope the great folks who drive the ambulances with patients who have to go to Halifax for emergency surgery are safe, along with their passengers.

Friendship and decorum

June 15, 2023

My dear friends—The Ladies Who Do Lunch—and I went to The Green Elephant in Kingston last week after what felt like a long time apart. We do call every now and then, and we do send photos and emails and messages, but it's just not the same.

We met like we hadn't talked for ages. We got caught up on the important bits. We shared some sad things. And some serious things. But mostly, we made a lot of noise and we laughed. A lot. And we hugged each other going into the restaurant and we hugged each other going out.

We are friends because we have some interests in common. Some of us have been friends longer than others. Not all of us have the same things in common but we do listen when someone brings a discussable subject to the table. We have been known to disagree with each other every now and then, but it sure is few and far between times.

I was thinking of this when I heard that David Johnston had resigned as the special rapporteur to look into foreign interference in Canadian elections. He will leave around the end of this month and will produce another report before he goes.

Prime Minister Stephen Harper recommended Mr. Johnston to Queen Elizabeth II in 2010 to be the Governor General. This was after a "special search committee" made a recommendation to the prime minister that Mr. Johnston was the man. I won't go through the membership of that search committee—have a look for yourself, if you like[19].

---

19   canada.ca/en/news/archive/2010/07/governor-general-consultation-committee.html

My point is that they were a mixed bag of politically savvy people and they looked at a list of over 200 people to take on the role of the queen's representative in Canada. I did not hear a whisper about Mr. Johnston's qualifications at that time. He did his duty with grace and kindness, I thought.

And look where we are now. Ten years on, with diatribes and nastiness and hurt heaped on this man's head by people who are much less than he is—nay, less than many of us are. We have come to this, my friends. If you want to get ahead in this new world, you speak with a wicked tongue, you slam another human being and you lie and you make things up about your fellow human.

I have been known to be critical of some politicians in my time. I don't think or recall that I ever lied about them. I criticized their actions or inactions. I said I didn't like them very much. Much of the time I said these things to the aforementioned friends over coffee or a sandwich.

I certainly did not blast away on television or radio about the personal life of someone because I was trying to make a point or get elected to be prime minister. Just because it's "politics" shouldn't give anyone the right to lie and slander and call into question another person's personal background.

Our leaders need to get a grip and listen to what us folks out here are saying. We want to hear them talk about real things, and do real things.

We elect those people to do things that will continue to make us glad to live in this rather remarkable country where five women of various ages can afford to go out to lunch once a month and share our hurts, our triumphs, our silly adventures, our embarrassments, our loves and our laughs right here in the Annapolis Valley of Nova Scotia.

Immediacy

June 29, 2023

I may have mentioned that I'm a news junkie—not always a flattering term, but I watch a lot of news on television, and I read a lot of news online.

Last Saturday was unbelievable. I was glued to the news channels watching the events in Russia, as the mercenary Wagner Group seemed to be on the verge of toppling the government headed by Vladimir Putin. Aside from the actual events, I was amazed at the speed we got what was going on almost as it was happening. I'll leave all the machinations and the implications of what happened to the experts. I do have a couple of opinions, but I'll leave punditry to others.[20]

We also watched and listened in horror to the news of that dreadful shipwreck in the Mediterranean Sea[21]. Those poor people who were trying to go somewhere else so they could have a life and being robbed to pay for an unbelievably awful escape route.

And then there was the submersible *Titan*, which imploded on its way to visit the wreck of the *Titanic*, with five rich folks on board[22]. There will be fallout from that episode, too.

And while all the above stories were certainly newsworthy, I was mostly struck by seeing and hearing about them almost immediately. The pictures and the reporters were on that screen with Breaking News right now.

I was thinking about the Reuters news article that appeared in *The Royal Gazette and Colonist* of Hamilton, Bermuda on Monday, February 12, 1945, telling the world that my Dad,

> wounded by flak after a strafing mission of Germany, thrown out of his cockpit and baling out into the slipstream, managed to drift back into the Allied lines and land on the doorstep of his favourite "pub" (tavern).

The event happened on January 16, 1945, so it took almost a month for the report to make it into the newspaper

I also thought about the time when I was watching TV in Chambly, Quebec, with my eldest daughter in her crib in the living room because she had a terrible case of chicken pox, I watched Walter Cronkite deliver the terrible news about President Kennedy having been assassinated in Texas. Then I saw Oswald being shot live on TV[23].

I was glued to the TV for the next three days, watching the news al-

---

20   aljazeera.com/news/2023/6/24/timeline-how-wagner-groups-revolt-against-russia-unfolded

21   wikipedia.org/wiki/2023_Messenia_migrant_boat_disaster

22   en.wikipedia.org/wiki/Titan_submersible_implosion

23   rarehistoricalphotos.com/jack-ruby-shot-oswald-1963/

most as it happened.

All the television coverage of the Vietnam War showed people back in the United States what war was really like almost as it happened, fuelling the anti-war movement that made that war end. I do realize that it wasn't quite as simple as that, but seeing those pictures every night on the tele-vision set certainly brought home how brutal war is.

I have over-simplified some of the above, but what we see nowadays is much more realistic and immediate than the reporting in the early part of the last century. But just because we can see and hear news sooner, doesn't make it any less horrific.

Freedom of the press

August 17, 2023

One person's newsletter I read every day is from Heather Cox Richard-son. She is an American historian who pays attention to the goings-on in that country and connects those events to their history.

Last week, Heather Historian (as we call her here) wrote about a small weekly newspaper in the middle of the Lower 48 of the US— the Marion County *Record* in Marion, Kansas. According to Ms. Richardson:

> Four local police officers and three sheriff's deputies raided the newspaper's office; the home of its co-owners, Eric Meyer and his 98-year-old mother, Joan Meyer; and the home of Marion vice mayor Ruth Herbel, 80. They seized computers, cell phones, and other equipment. Joan Meyer was unable to eat or sleep after the raid; she collapsed Saturday afternoon and died at her home.

The story gets quite complicated, with reporters thrown out of a meet-ing, mudslinging on the part of a restaurant owner and on and on. Ms. Richardson gives more details in her newsletter of August 12, 2023, should you wish to know more[24].

---

24 heathercoxrichardson.substack.com/p/august-12-2023

I have worked for a number of news outlets over time—The Bridge-water *Bulletin, The 4th ESTATE* (a paper with a point of view), the CBC, *News of the North*—and have seen and heard threats from people who didn't want the public to know about something they did which was wrong. Any "controversial" stories or articles had to be checked and veri-fied in detail before they went to press or on the air. Getting things right was always front of mind. I was always well aware that anything in print was going to last in some form or other for the future.

Some of the mainstream media is being lumped in with some very scummy voices out there. There is news, there is commentary, there are experts with deeper knowledge of a subject; but not everyone you read, hear or see is giving you the best information. Listen, read or watch very carefully. "Know the source" is a great caution.

Once you have found a news source you trust, stick with it. Support them if you can, by subscribing. Reputable news organizations are be-coming rare. It's fine to have "freedom of the press" as long as there's a free press out there.

My uncle owned and edited a weekly newspaper in rural Ontario. He would have been appalled at the situation in Marion, Kansas. Pay atten-tion to rural weekly newspapers—they are becoming scarcer and scarcer.

Your Facebook posts and online thoughts and notices and information may not last for the next 100 years. They could be scrubbed as fast as a speeding bullet. Don't count on those thoughts being a "scrapbook" of your life for the next generations.

One more random thought today: with the fires raging and the waters rising and a new COVID-19 variant possibly mowing down more people, remember that if things don't change in a real hurry, humans will be gone, but the earth will not.

Gaia will heal herself once she has sloughed off the vermin that have thoughtlessly tried to kill her.

Bank closures hit rural communities

November 16, 2023

One of the big topics around these parts is banks. There was a meeting at the Bridgetown Fire Hall on Tuesday, held by the Valley Credit Union. I will be interested to see what the community has to say.

The reason for this recent banking kerfuffle is the announcement that the branches of ScotiaBank in both Bridgetown and Annapolis Royal are going to shut down next year. The closure of the Royal Bank in Bridgetown earlier this year has been added to the discussion.

I thought I would have a look at the history of these banks—where they started and what they've been doing over the years.

Let's start with The Bank of Nova Scotia. It was incorporated by the Legislative Assembly of Nova Scotia on March 30, 1832, in Halifax. From that point until 2003, the bank took over 17 other banks and institutions of money and acquired big shares in seven other institutions of money. Ten of those banks were not Canadian. As an aside, did you know that there is a real Canadian Tire Bank? I didn't. ScotiaBank has a 20% stake in it.

The Royal Bank of Canada was founded in Halifax in 1864. From that date to last year, it engaged in buying and selling over 50 banking institutions all over the world, from the Caribbean to Australia, South America, Europe, Asia and the United States. It's a very long list. And some of the list follows history, i.e. the Cuban Revolution and the US-backed Bay of Pigs assault on Cuba. We now know it as RBC, and the Bridgetown branch closed recently.

The Valley Credit Union has seven branches—in Bridgetown, Middleton, Greenwood, Cambridge, New Minas, Canning and Hantsport. The Head Office is in Waterville.

Here are just a few of the Credit Union "firsts" in Canada:

- First Canadian financial institution to lend women money in their own name (in the 1960s)
- First full-service ABMs
- First debit card service

After going through all the research on the above three money institutions, it seems to me that the first two got out of looking after the small clients—both individuals and small businesses—pretty quickly. They started there in the early 1800s and then moved to the Big Cities and then out into the world. And all the decisions are made in the big towers in Montreal and Toronto.

When these branches close to save money for the shareholders, there is local damage done with local people losing jobs—good jobs. That part of the economy is lost.

The fact that most of these rural branches look after CPP and OAS deposits either digitally or by real cheques is not very big potatoes for them. Especially when they are busy looking after Argentina or Hong Kong or Austria or Belize.

It has been said already, but an older population lives in rural Canada. They sometimes live far from any bank branch and make a weekly trip to town to get groceries, pick up mail, go to the pharmacy, go to the library and go to the bank to pick up cash or pay a bill or cash a cheque. Many older people do not have computers or cell phones. They do not do online banking. Many older people still pay with cash.

Those who still need to see someone real to do banking stuff will not be happy having to drive to Kingston or Digby to go to "their bank" that they have used all their lives. And the name Nova Scotia holds loyalty to folks here as well.

By the way, it is an education to look up the history of the banking industry. Hair-raising, in fact.

Wanderers and explorers

June 22, 2023

When I disembarked from Cunard's ship the *Scythia II* in June of 1945 at Pier 21 with my mother, the population of Canada was about 12 million.

Just imagine: in a country with nearly 10 million square kilometres, there was just over one person per square kilometre. Yes, I know they were in bunches here and there in this country, but still...

The population has been growing—13.8 million in 1950; 24.5 million in 1980 and now we have reached 40 million. And the recent growth has been largely due to immigration. Birth rates are falling.

I remember a time when families were made up of two parents and five children. Mine was, and it was not unusual. It seems that nowadays couples have one or possibly two children.

On to other things. I belong to the Annapolis Heritage Society (AHS) here in Annapolis Royal. For three long, dark years during COVID-19, life has been difficult for many of the small museums around the province. I won't list all the reasons—I'm sure you know why. Our museum has also been through the weather wars with leaks and some roof repairs required. It has been very trying.

We are not unique in being a small, local museum. What we are is the repository of the history of this part of Canada. The information, the documents, the photographs, the genealogical records, the furniture, the bits and bobs of begone times live at the O'Dell House Museum. We are also responsible for the Sinclair Inn, in the middle of downtown Annapolis Royal. You can see its history on the AHS website[25].

We are the caretaker, on behalf of the province of Nova Scotia, of the North Hills Museum in Granville Ferry, with its beautiful collection of antiques.

These three buildings tell stories of a past that was bustling and wealthy and world-wise. They combine with Parks Canada's Fort Anne, Melanson Settlement, and Port Royal Habitation to tell the stories from a

---

25   annapolisheritagesociety.com

long time ago up to the late Victorian era.

And we are paying much more attention these days to the people who lived in this area before the Europeans decided to come here. We certainly need to be mindful of the Peace and Friendship Treaty of 1752[26].

It feels like that great grey mass of three years has dissipated and we are awakening, with events happening and places opening up.

And as all this information is floating around in my mind, it seems to me that human beings are wanderers and explorers and, yes, refugees from all over the world. People fill up some spaces and empty others. I expect this will be happening even more as the weather changes and makes some parts of the Earth unlivable.

Our huge land mass needs to be welcoming. We certainly have the space.

A letter to Nova Scotia Power

September 28, 2023

Dear Nova Scotia Power,

I thought I would dash off a quick note to tell you—in case you haven't noticed—that the storms are increasing in intensity and number, and we aren't even through with hurricane season. And, in case you haven't noticed, we are now officially in autumn. That means winter will be coming next.

I happen to be in the land of the four-leafed clover, or the place where there is magic in the air. All the horrible weather has not hit us here in Annapolis Royal this past year. We didn't get hit with Fiona. We didn't get any forest fires. We didn't get floods, and Lee gave us some rain and some wind but that's all. I don't mind telling you that saying all this makes me a bit nervous. I feel like I might be jinxing this place.

Anyway, here's what I want you to know: having power failures all over the place is just not good enough in the 21st century. I have listened

---

26   thecanadianencyclopedia.ca/en/article/peace-and-friendship-treaties

with patience to the various spokespeople from your office saying how you've put in 100 new generators for the cell towers. And I also heard that you have been on a tree pruning tear around the province.

I know of one part of my town that has no wires on poles. It's a new part, and I expect the developers paid a pretty penny to get the lines installed, but I don't know about that.

But doesn't it make sense to start—on your own volition—putting your power cables in the ground and sharing the cost of burying lines with the phone and internet folks?

The poles are going to continue coming down in strong winds. Trees are going to take down wires. Those transformers waving away in the wind could be on the ground in a box, which would make them a lot easier to service or to add a new customer.

We had visitors here from Europe a week or so ago and they were marvelling at all the overhead wires in Canada.

I won't start up about getting out of the fossil-fuel racket—you've heard the din out here. Get on with it.

You have to understand that the general populace is not exactly fond of you, especially when they read that the shareholders are getting a bit of a raise. And here at home, the general populace doesn't really care to hear that your bosses at Emera are spending their time and efforts looking after Tampa, Florida and a couple of other faraway places.

I'm sure you have heard the folks out here saying things like, "We never should have sold the Nova Scotia Power Commission in 1992. It should have stayed a Crown Corporation."

In closing, I would like to say that things aren't going to get any better in the Weather and Acts of God Department. They are probably going to get worse.

So get on your horses and make these things happen before the Big Things happen.

Sincerely
Anne M. Crossman

A response to a response

November 2, 2023

Dear Peter Gregg,
President and CEO
Nova Scotia Power

Thank you for your return email of October 23, 2023 regarding reliability of service and your remarks about burying the power cables[27]. I was pleased to see that you "continue working with municipalities and developers to install underground systems, where it makes sense, and we're always looking for opportunities to bury more lines."

I was also pleased to hear that "the infrastructure to charge electric vehicles is largely under-ground". You did go on to say that burying the present infrastructure would be about ten times more expensive.

I was also wondering who owns the poles that carry all kinds of wire and transistors and transformers and cable extenders and connectors that one can see along the roads and highways here.

I assumed that Bell Canada had some part to play in the wiring.

It turns out that NS Power and Bell own the poles jointly, according to Katie Hatfield of Bell Aliant. She was kind enough to get back to me in response to my question. She added that "all telecommunications providers have access to the utility poles."

Ms. Hatfield added, "Moving existing utility lines underground is extremely costly and complex. If a developer opts to have power and communications services run underground, they would fund the construction of the required infrastructure during the development of the roads according to the utilities' standards."

And she said, "Bell is moving to an all-fibre network and gradually upgrading copper components. In Atlantic Canada, copper theft is most common in New Brunswick where Bell has experienced more than 115 incidents of network vandalism (mostly copper theft) since January

---

27   See the previous essay.

2022."

And so we have answers to most of the questions, but I still think that more work needs to be done to get that vital infrastructure safely tucked away so that it is not as vulnerable to the kind of deadly situations we are finding ourselves in as a result of climate change[28].

On behalf of your NS Power and Bell customers, I appreciate your time and I know that if I have any more questions, you will get back to me.

Sincerely,
Anne Crossman

An uncertain ferry

November 30, 2023

If you happen to live somewhere in Annapolis Royal or Annapolis County, the name Rose Fortune will be more than familiar to you. This woman of another time is a hero around here.

According to a detailed article on the Annapolis Heritage Society's website, she is likely the only child aged 'over 10 years' of parents "Fortune and wife", listed as "Free Negroes" in the muster roll taken at Annapolis Royal in June of 1783. We do know that Rose was buried in the Garrison Cemetery at Fort Anne and that she was about 90 when she died.

Rose worked hard and built a business as a luggage carrier between the wharf and various businesses and hotels in town. She passed that business along to her family and it was still going, albeit more modern than the wheelbarrow this doughty lady used, until 1960. I am quite certain she would have been very proud of one of her descendants, Daurene Lewis, who became the first Black Mayor in Canada when she was elected Mayor of Annapolis Royal in the 1980s.

---

28 During tropical storm Don on July 21-22, 2023, Nova Scotia saw a record 23,008 lightning strikes—more than triple the historical average for the full month of July, according to Nova Scotia Power. - *AllNovaScotia*

There is much more to this woman's story which is worth checking out.

And so when it came time to name the new ferry going between Digby and Saint John, what more fitting name to put on the motor vessel than "Fundy Rose", commemorating a strong business woman, Rose Fortune, whose business was tied to shipping over 200 years ago?

There has been a ferry service between Digby and Saint John for over 200 years. And before that, the trading vessels left from Bridgetown, picking up apples along the river at small wharves and then sailing on to the big wharf at Annapolis Royal, and from there across the Bay of Fundy to Saint John.

The ferry services now are operated under license by the federal Department of Transportation, which lives in Ottawa. The department is "considering" moving the MV Fundy Rose over to serve the crossing from PEI to the Magdalen Islands for a couple of months while that ferry is in for refit. I don't know about you, but my ears perked up at "a couple of months". We all know what that means.

For a week or so, the municipalities sent emails off to complain and make their case. Crickets! Now I see that our Nova Scotia Minister of Public Works has chimed in, and that's great. Small aside here: she apparently had to hear this possibility from her constituents, not the feds.

And so, where does all this get us? As of early this week—nowhere.

So once again, the high hand of someone in Ottawa says, "Gee, we have to get that ferry refitted that goes to Quebec's Magdalen Islands. We'd better find a replacement for a couple of months or so. Let's have a look at our map and see if there's one close that we can just pop right in that slot—no problem. How about that one over there in the Bay of Fundy? They won't mind."

And what do we get back from Pablo Rodriguez, the federal Minister of Transportation? "He's looking forward to meeting with officials on this issue."

It's a head-shaker and much more than a bit aggravating. I can imagine a few fists being raised.[29]

---

29 In December, 2023, the federal Transport Minister announced that MV Fundy Rose would not be moved to the PEI-Magdalen Islands route after all.

Homelessness in the County

December 14, 2023

I have lived in a tent twice in my life. I'm not talking about camping, although I've done a fair amount of that.

I am talking about setting up a tent to live in because we couldn't find a place to live because we couldn't afford the rent because we were part of a strange group of working poor.

The first time living in a tent was in a field, from where I went to work as a waitress. You all remember saying to yourself, "Oh well, if I lose my job, I can always be a waitress." Let me tell you, my respect for wait-people is still extremely high. It's a hard job, both physically and psychologically.

The second time was not quite as dire, but it was still a tent...this time with a wood stove in it. Living in it in winter, with an outdoor privy and a swish barrel, was only fun for a few weeks, and we stayed there for a few months.

Both times may have built my character, but when I look back on those times, I think the two best parts were telling the stories afterwards and knowing that I could do it.

A recent report about current and projected housing needs for each of the 49 municipalities in Nova Scotia is being examined to determine if those needs are going to be met. I will dwell on Annapolis Royal and Annapolis County here.

There were surveys sent out to local residents, apparently, and although only 20 people responded from Annapolis Royal, the firms working on this provincial project (UPLAND, Turner Drake, CoLab and MountainMath) felt the need in this town is 120 new units by 2027 (including the existing shortage of 60) and 155 by 2032.

When it comes to the County, the firms say,

> that Projections suggest that to keep pace with population growth, the municipality will need 2,005 new units by 2027 (in-

cluding the existing shortage of 1,015) and 2,575 by 2032.

There is an interesting project being touted by the Cornwallis Park Development Association. There is a lot of information on their website; the gist of it is to develop the old Cornwallis training base into an affordable housing space, and developing the disused site in Annapolis Royal where the cadets learned about boating.

The Cornwallis Park lands include 55 acres bordering the Annapolis Basin. The Annapolis Royal lands include 10.8 acres bordering the Annapolis River.

So it's fine to have all the above statistics and prognostications, but do we know how many people need affordable housing here now? There are houses being lived in that haven't had decent upgrading for 50 years or more. They need plumbing and proper wiring and new roofing and new heating systems of some sort. All those renovations take money— cold, hard cash. The people in those buildings are one step above living in a tent, and they don't have that kind of money for housing upgrades, on top of their everyday needs.

We have had a brief uptick in properties being sold and bought. Some of those, after some fixing, became short-term rental units which would cost far more for a local family on social assistance to be living in.

Most of the news these days is on the homeless living in tents and/or ice fishing shacks in Halifax and Dartmouth. What about our people here who are in need? I know they are out there, and are probably more numerous than we assume.

We have to do better, my neighbours. We have to look after our own folks in some warm and generous fashion. Please remember to ask these questions of those running for office when the next bunch of elections come along.

Heritage

When we moved back to Nova Scotia in 1998, we had choices to make. The first question was, "What could our money buy?" The second question was, "Where?"

My husband is from Cape Breton, and he said he wanted a milder winter than there. I really liked the idea of living in someplace called Annapolis Royal or even Annapolis County. I guess my first name says it all. Having lived in parts of Canada which had colonial history back only a century or so ago, living in an area that went back almost four centuries really appealed to me.

I became involved in a few organizations which had heritage as their main focus, and it has been a great time of discovery for me.

Anne Crossman's

Make your own map

February 11, 2021

I believe I come by my fascination with maps honestly. My grandfather, J. Leslie Rannie, was Canada's Dominion Geodesist in 1951, when he was appointed Commissioner "to define and mark the boundary line between the United States of America and Canada in accordance with the terms of the said Treaty" signed in 1903.

While Grandpa Rannie didn't go on those treks to do the work, I believe he was the last Commissioner. The boundary is the squiggly one between British Columbia and Alaska that goes from just north of Prince Rupert to Mount St. Elias.

I have been making maps with Google Maps for some years now. The biggest project was for Mapannapolis[30] in 2012. A small group got together and, with the help of instructors and students at COGS (Centre for Geographic Sciences) in Lawrencetown, put together a map of as many heritage buildings built before 1914 in Annapolis County, Annapolis Royal, Bridgetown and Middleton as we could find. We know that every property isn't there.

This really was a labour of love for me. I can't count the number of hours I spent trying to get each little house on the right spot on the map.

I remember going to COGS every week or so and learning just like the students were. We taught them and they taught us. I always say that I got a "certificate" in mapping for seniors during that time. I know we had a great time and I sure hope they enjoyed it, too.

We asked the good folks at the Annapolis County offices to let us borrow their big binders with the work done by various industrious people in the 1980s and 1990s. They filled in documents called Inventory Site Forms. The front of each entry had a photo, the type of architecture, and any stories about the property, and on the back there was a history of the builder and owners. That work was huge and I am so grateful to both the

---

30 mapannapolis.ca

County of Annapolis and the provincial government for funding that work.

I entered over 2,500 properties on that map. It also includes some churches and a few cemeteries. The oldest on the map is, of course, the DeGannes-Cosby house, in Annapolis Royal. But there are some real oldies around.

I live in a house built in 1866 by Alfred Messinger. He owned the property until 1909. His son, Alf, owned the property until 1975. He had a market garden behind the house and used to go in his truck, selling produce, down past Annapolis Royal.

Apparently, he had a bullhorn through which he told his customers he was in the area. And when he hit the home stretch, he would let his wife know (publicly) and ask her to put the kettle on. In his later years, Alf was blind, but he still managed to weed his garden by using baling twine tied to various objects in the backyard as a guide so he could even weed at night.

There is more to this story, but the point I want to make is that making a map of where you live is like reading a book of peoples' life stories.

Back to Grandpa Rannie: he did a lot of surveying of Canada's wilderness. There used to be a lake in Labrador called Rannie Lake, but it was flooded out when the big Churchill Falls hydro dam project opened in 1974. And there is a Rannie township in western Quebec named after him.

One of his best stories took place during World War II. He was surveying on Southampton Island in the far north. There is a great photo of him standing next to a surveying cairn that has a whale skull on the top. He is wearing a beret with the initial "W" on it, signifying he was an Air Raid Precautions (ARP) Division Warden (back in Ottawa actually). You had to do double-duty when you were a federal civil servant during the war. Grandpa was also a bit of a jokester!

If you ask me, "Where have you lived?", I made a Google Earth map to show you. It's pretty impressive, but not nearly as impressive as some I know. I also made a map to show all the places I have visited.

So, for those of you who are sick of knitting, crocheting, stamp collecting or breadmaking during this Time Of COVID, you might want to consider making your own maps. It whiles away the time wonderfully and brings back lots of memories.

Very old houses

March 11, 2021

Buying an old house is not for the faint of heart. It could actually be better to purchase one that has been "fixed". It depends on how strong your marital relationship is. If you are single and young-ish and strong and have money, that might work.

But the rewards are wonderful.

I tend to think of some of the old houses here in Annapolis County as history containers. The stories they hold could tell about the people who lived in them over time...

Some houses are old enough to have kept a number of generations safe from the storm. I think of those who may have been born in the bedroom upstairs. There would have been laughter and tears. There would have been dinners with lots on the table and sometimes the table fare would have been a bit sparse.

And I think of how these buildings have stood up to weather beyond belief. My sort of favourite is the Saxby Gale of October 4–5, 1869. I say "sort of" only because I'm glad I wasn't here yet. The house I live in was built in 1866 so, as it was standing up here on the hill, it would have taken a proper pounding.

There are the fireplaces. You know the ones, with bricks and big enough for a small person to stand inside. There were cooking fireplaces and the heating fireplaces and the holes in the wall that had stovepipes connected to them.

There were the lovely old wooden mouldings for the doors and windows that were made either in Bridgetown or even down at Roney's near Port Wade. And there were the mantelpieces that were made for the different fireplaces around the house.

There is no certainty that there were dogs and/or cats which were allowed to park in front of those fireplaces but I like to think that, especially on a cold winter's day, they were there. I know that's where our dog likes to be, until it gets a tad too warm and she wanders off.

There were chimneys made with brick. Before all the refinements and safety considerations that we have today, these could produce chimney fires that would scare the heck out of you. If you get the idea that I have seen one, I have. Not in this house, though, thank goodness.

I understand that setting fire to the inside of the chimney in the spring was a good way to get rid of the creosote buildup. I never want to be near one of those roaring infernos again. Thank goodness for the metal chimney here.

A friend suggested I get a copy of *Seasoned Timbers, Vol. 1*, published by The Heritage Trust of Nova Scotia in 1972. It gives a sampling of the historic buildings unique to southwest Nova Scotia. It is a gem, with a section on Annapolis County for which I am grateful.

We have living history here in Annapolis County and I hope we can remember and celebrate these lovely old buildings, which have given shelter to so many over these past hundreds of years.

And just because we are in 2021, those two days of wind and cold this past week reminded us what it must have been like decades ago. It meant we shut room doors and stayed mostly in the room with the fireplace—just like they did years and years ago.

In praise of museums

June 3, 2021

A week or so ago, museums across the country gave themselves a day. These small community keepers of the history and heritage of their place are so important to the depth of understanding of how we got here and the why we chose this as our home.

There are big museums and small ones. I have been to many big history/heritage museums and big art museums and have stood in awe at the accomplishments of humankind. I have been fortunate to hear the stories of elders who keep the history of their people alive.

I am particularly fond of the small museums. They seem more homey to me. They tell the stories of ordinary folk. There might very well be some stars of history celebrated among the exhibits, but these museums are run by people who are really interested in the genealogy of the place, the small triumphs over adversity, the skilled workmanship, the making a living off the land and the sea that helped people survive in small communities.

I live where people used both the sea and the land to make a living. There still is some farming going on; there are the orchards, there are the small business folks who work like the dickens—especially in this Time of COVID—to make a living for their families and their employees. And the museums keep those stories in the form of old newspapers and photographs and bits and bobs of things that folks of yore believed were important enough to preserve.

In my area, there are three museums to which I pay attention. There is the Macdonald Museum in Middleton, the James House Museum in Bridgetown and the Annapolis Heritage Society's three facilities—the O'Dell House Museum and the Sinclair Inn Museum, both in Annapolis Royal, and the North Hills Museum in Granville Ferry. Go to their websites to see when they are open and if they have any special exhibits. The Macdonald Museum has a related Market in the warm part of the year.

If you live in a community that is lucky enough to have one of these gems, do give a thought to joining and helping out and, if nothing else—when the lockdowns are lifted and we are able to be sociable again—go and see what stories these places have to tell.

Pier 21

July 22, 2021

As many of us are immigrants to this part of world, it is interesting to look back and see both where we came from and how we got here.

Over the years, I have done our family tree entries. That tree has gotten a little large (2,777 people) as I included relatives of relatives of relatives, but the process has been quite fascinating. I did the DNA test as well. I know there are those who get a bit twisted about having so much personal information "out there", but it doesn't bother me very much. The connections are fun and, in my case, are all over the world.

One of the close-to-home places for information about me is actually in Halifax, right down there on the waterfront: Pier 21. That's where I first entered Canada. My mother went to England to marry my father, who had gone over to join the Royal Air Force. I was born in Chester.

My father came back to Canada in February, 1945. In June, after the war was over, my mother and I made the trip. We landed in Halifax on board the *Scythia*. I was able to see the information about that ship at Pier 21.

One of the things that really bothers me about all this is that I have no memory at all of that grand voyage. I don't remember going on the train from Chester to Liverpool or boarding the *Scythia* (with 2,000 other passengers) or sailing across the ocean or landing in Halifax at Pier 21 or taking the train to Ottawa—nothing, not a scrap or a smidgen. As I age, I find that my brain's memory file drawers are pretty full and sometimes things slip down behind the filing cabinet, never to be found again.

It's worth going to the Pier 21 website and reading the stories of those who entered Canada through that big building. There are people who fled a terrible situation in their home country; there are those who came for economic reasons—a way to get ahead; there are those who already had relatives here; there are those who chose Canada as a possible gateway to the United States; and there are those who came because they thought Canada looked like a big, peaceful, country with lots of land.

Last year, two of the staff at the Canadian Museum of Immigration published *Pier 21: a history*, a book that gives a history of the building itself and then tells the stories of some remarkable people who passed through it. It's those tales of families coming in past George's Island over time that are the most interesting to me. The one I liked best is:

> Customs officer Marguerite Day took one jar of preserved meat from its Italian owner, which dismayed and upset the man. After repeated protests, it came to light that he had packed a fair amount of American currency in a condom inside the jar.

I must also say that the folks who work there are the best. They are help-ful and knowledgeable.

Rural built heritage

August 12, 2021

There was a letter to the editor in *The Chronicle Herald* last week from a person lamenting the loss of Halifax's history, its "elderly, elegant buildings of brick, sandstone and wood."

It reminded me of a meeting I attended a number of years ago at the Hotel Nova Scotian, which was made up of heritage folks from around the province. As I sat there listening to the city planner session, I looked out the window and all I could see was glass and steel and ruler-straight lines.

I didn't see the wonderful old Pickford & Black building on the corner of Duke and Hollis streets, where I worked on the second floor. The ceiling was at least 16 feet high, and it was one of those lovely tin ones. There were big windows and we looked across at one of the old red stone buildings with rounded windows on the corner with rounded glass (it's still there, now an RBC building). It was fascinating to me how they did that.

My old workplace has been replaced with one of those glass-and-metal constructions.

So the letter-writer's lament struck a chord with me. And it made me wonder if rural Nova Scotia has managed to do a better job of preserving its built heritage. I do know that we celebrate it here in Annapolis County.

Yes, there have been some small griefs—a church from here was sold by the Anglican Diocese a number of years ago and is somewhere in the southern United States, serving a congregation there. The Troop Octagonal Barn was sold and moved to Lunenburg County.

But on the whole, people seem to like the grand old homes and some of the more modest old homes, and have updated them inside and kept the lines of the outside looking as they did all those years ago of ships and long ocean voyages, which made this place fairly wealthy.

The home I live in was originally built in 1866, the year before Confederation. When we bought it 23 years ago, work had been started to renovate it. We bought a shell with a new basement. It had been stripped to the bones.

Luckily for us, they had saved all the trim and baseboards and windows. There was birch bark "Tyvek" and evidence of a small fire on one of the wall beams upstairs. Basically, the house had to be rebuilt from the outside in.

Of course, this is work that never ends, but I am glad we were able to keep this old home on the hill from disappearing. I would recommend the 'Saving Abandoned Nova Scotia' Facebook page, curated by Bridgetown-area Steve Skafte, for tips and success stories.

We take our built heritage seriously here in Annapolis County. We have a Heritage Advisory Committee, which meets when a property owner wishes to have a municipal heritage designation or wishes to make some modification to a presently-designated building. The people who want to go through this process obviously care about their acquisition. They see the value of preserving our history through these buildings. They learn the stories of the people who lived there before them and wish to add to that book of stories.

The Annapolis River, the Rivière du Dauphin, is a storied place, too, with its history of shipbuilding and wharves. And there are the *aboiteaus* built by the Acadians all those centuries ago in the dikes along the river. There are Acadian house foundations still hiding in properties around here.

It seems as if the Halifax developers are more interested in tearing something down and putting up a replacement with no soul, no storied past. And it appears that the city fathers are letting them.

So if people in Halifax are wishing for a large dose of heritage, come on over. We are happy to have you point and say things like, "Isn't that charming!"

A town reinvented and books galore

October 21, 2021

Sometime back in the 1960s, my family went on an excursion to Annapolis Royal. We stayed at the Champlain Motel, where the Searidge Foundation rehabilitation centre is now on Highway 1 on the west side of the town. There was fishing for striped bass, a trip to the Habitation and a visit to the town. It was a weekend, and the only place open was a very small "corner" store.

The Annapolis River was wonderful and the Habitation was very interesting, but Annapolis Royal certainly didn't live up to its name. There was nothing "royal" about it.

Move through the years to the formation of the Annapolis Royal Development Commission in 1976. The vision of some of the people was, "We can't let this town die or collapse." It's the oldest town in Canada, for goodness' sake!

I read Jason Malloy's story in the October 13 *Register* with great interest. I was sorry not to be able to go to King's Theatre to see the film. But now we can all see the documentary on YouTube[31]. It does exactly what it was meant to do—show how a committed group of citizens can get together and make things happen.

A friend said the other day, "There are people who should watch this film". I agree. I think it should be mandatory viewing for any municipal elected official to see how working together in a positive way with a view to the future makes a good life for all.

PS – I am a local bookophile. If a neighbour has taken the time to "tell" stories about their time in this area or about something that took place here and actually put those treasures in a book—I want it. I have quite a few and another one walked in my door last week: *An Eggplant, a Starr, and a Pony Walk Into a Cafe*, by my great friend Chantelle Webb.

---

31   youtube.com/watch?v=0rABIJhdMck

Chantelle tells you right off the bat that she is a "serial entrepreneur". She makes me feel dizzy and sloth-like! This latest book can be had locally.

I also recommend anything Paul Colville writes. He has the great fortune to live on Delusion Road! His book is called *The View from Delusion Road*. That always sounds like the place I should have lived.

There are many more, and we have a publisher in these parts as well —Moose House Publications—and a printer—Integrity Printing. I am exactly where I should be: in the middle of a group of library-fillers!

Bridgetown reborn

December 9, 2021

I live close to Bridgetown. I have watched its trials and tribulations and its amazing tenacity over the past 20 years.

I saw its gradual decline when the rules changed for small communities' water supplies after the terrible Walkerton E. coli outbreak in 2000. More than 2,000 people in Walkerton became ill and six people died. The bill for the new town water supply was gargantuan for a municipality the size of Bridgetown.

Things got so bad financially that there was a decision to basically disband the town's status and merge it with Annapolis County. Although there was some complaining about the situation, it went relatively smoothly, much to many people's surprise.

And then there was a period of a kind of mourning. A time when people weren't really sure how it was going to work.

Small businesses had the Bridgetown and Area Chamber of Commerce, and they really got going on a number of projects. That organization had spark plugs! They just went ahead and did stuff, boldly.

Of course, there's the big new school, which I understand is filled to capacity. I've been in there and it really is something.

There's the Sports Hub, which looks fantastic even if sprinting and all that other exercise stuff doesn't appeal to me. And there's the chimney swifts' chimney, which is delightful.

As you can see, I've started moving into the positive stuff. There are folks in this town who just don't seem to be able to give up. There's a lovely new sign at the parking lot side of the Town Hall.

Dawn Oman's church (that's what I call it) continues to be a vibrant part of the community, with music and art and crafts and just plain presence.

There are new owners of the Bridgetown Motor Inn who seem to be fitting in just fine. They have had a couple of community events already which have brought some new energy to the place.

There are all kinds of new families moving in, with lots of kiddoes! That always livens up a place and does a few other things as well. These new folks contribute to the economy, they bring new ideas, they bring new small businesses, they ask questions about what is available, possibly prompting someone to start up something new. And the community has welcomed them all with open arms and bags of goodies and information about the place.

While the Christmas Season is proving a bit difficult, what with the Time of COVID, anything that can be done safely is being done—what great work, Bridgetown folks!

Hillsdale House Inn

April 14, 2022

The Hillsdale House Inn in Annapolis Royal has changed hands once again. This will be the fourth time since I've been in these parts.

I have some very fond memories which took place in this lovely old yellow place sitting on the spacious grounds that go all the way down to Allain's Creek. Hillsdale House was built in 1859 by Susan Forbes Foster. It became an inn about ten years afterwards. The Annapolis Royal historian Charlotte Perkins was an owner at one point.

It has had some high-falutin' guests over time—Prince George (later King George V), Lord and Lady Lansdowne, Governor General Lord Tweedsmuir, and Prime Minister William Lyon Mackenzie King.

According to local lore, Susan's sister Fanny wanted a more elaborate home than her sister and had her husband, William Ritchie, build the house now known as the Queen Anne Inn right across St. George Street. The building put them in serious debt, and it was opened as an elite boarding house.

While all that was long ago, my memories are of a lovely dinner with my sister-in-law, her husband and my husband on our 20th actual wedding anniversary. We told them over dinner that we were heading back up to Inuvik for a couple of years.

And there was the time my family had a reunion. Almost all of them stayed at the Hillsdale. There are lots of photos. And the Town Crier, Peter Davies, greeted us all at breakfast the next morning, ringing his bell.

There was the Mad Hatter Tea where my great friend and I went with our snazzy hats and sat out in the garden amongst the members of the Red Hat Society, who never missed a good tea.

There were Christmas gift exchanges held there with friends, and barbecues in the summer. When the tourist season was over, a bunch of us women would get together to relax and tell tales and get to stay overnight in one of the lovely rooms. That was a rare treat!

There used to be an organization that brought musicians to small house parties. The most memorable for me was listening to Nathan Rogers, Stan Rogers' son. I hesitated to ask him if he got tired of being compared to his father. He said that it didn't bother him now, but it had in the past. Then he realized that he had his own songs to sing, and he did—beautifully. He also sang some of Stan's, though, and as I looked around the parlour at Hillsdale (through tears), I saw others a bit weepy as well. A good songwriter and performer will do that to you.

The hosts over the years were (and are) dear friends. I still go to gatherings where we tell tales and get caught up on our lives—especially during the Time of COVID. There are the same old jobs, the new jobs, the jobs left behind, the present political situation in Canada, the political situation in the US, the dreadful war in Ukraine, who has had COVID in the community, and it's a good thing we all tested ourselves before getting together.

And so the venerable Hillsdale House Inn will continue its long life of making memories for many others down the years.

Monuments and plaques

April 21, 2022

I learned the other day that the Pony Express in the US started in April 1860 and eventually ran between California and the East Coast. It only lasted 18 months, however. It is certainly the backdrop to many Western films over the years. It was eventually replaced by the transcontinental telegraph.

It reminded me that we had our own version of the Pony Express here in Nova Scotia, and that it started before the American one. Between February and November 1849, the Associated Press financed the ride from Halifax to Digby Gut, where the dispatches from Europe were shipped to the Saint John telegraph station. Those dispatches were then sent to the American news outlets. The plaque in Victoria Beach says that the ride from Halifax to Digby Gut took as little as eight hours—146 miles—with fresh horses changed along the route and rider changes at Kentville. This Pony Express was replaced when the telegraph reached Halifax.

There are all kinds of interesting historic bits and bobs around the province that are commemorated by plaques and monuments. We have quite a few notable events, people and even animals here in Annapolis County. Since the weather seems to be getting to the point where outside activities could be planned, I thought it might be time to visit some of these sites. It might also be a good time to remind ourselves about the rich history that happened here.

While Fritz (a war horse) and Bruno (a sheepdog) may not have a plaque, they are memorable because they were great buddies from World War I who were brought back to Paradise to live out their lives with Lieutenant-Colonel Charles Bent, commanding officer of the 15th Battalion (48th Highlanders).

Another local worthy was Gertrude 'Gert' Ritchie. She was born in Annapolis Royal and passed away there. She lived quite a life in between. She was in the Royal Canadian Air Force Women's Division (RCAFWD) and worked as a clerk and equipment assistant during World War II. She worked in the business world before working for Parks Canada at Fort Anne and the Alexander Graham Bell National Historic Site in Baddeck.

Many know of Rose Fortune, daughter of a Black Loyalist family in the American colonies who eventually became a successful entrepreneur in Annapolis Royal. She is commemorated there on the corner of St. George and Church streets with a plaque. She lived between 1774 and 1864.

Annapolis Royal has its own Historic District—St. George Street. There is quite a long story on the plaque on the corner of St. George and St. James streets. But then, this town has a very long history, starting with the Mi'kmaq, and then the French in 1605. After that it exchanged hands between the French and the English many times.

Within the confines of little Annapolis Royal is the Annapolis County Court House, which I see is being fixed up these days. It is one of the oldest courthouses in Canada, built in 1837, and is still in use today.

Within Annapolis Royal, at the Fort Anne grounds, are a whole bunch of plaques and monuments to people like Charles de Menou d'Aulnay; Samuel Vetch; Admiral Philipps Cosby; Sir William Alexander; William Wolseley; Colonel Jean-Paul Mascarene; and Pierre Dugua, Sieur de Mons. There are some fascinating buildings and structures there as well. It is hoped that Alan Melanson will once again be conducting his candlelight tours of the graveyard this year.

Did you know that the Schafner Point Lighthouse is a heritage building? It's the one on Granville Road going out towards Port Royal. It was built in 1885. I believe it is undergoing some restoration these days.

There's the Bloody Creek National Historic Site on Highway 201, just after Centrelea. The next time you head to Bridgetown on the 201, stop and have a look at the plaque on the cairn there[32].

There's the lovely, restored Heritage Railway Station in Annapolis Royal, built in 1915. It is used now as an office. One can imagine the passengers going to faraway places starting here. There would also be newcomers arriving to a new home.

And then there's Port Royal Habitation. I still go there and look out across the water, squint my eyes a bit and imagine the lovely sailing ships coming up the basin into the river. The people who tell the story of the Habitation are really good, and it's truly worth a visit.

Just up the road from the Habitation is the Melanson Settlement site. It was started in 1664 and lasted until the Acadian Deportation in 1755.

There are far more details about all these people and places around

---

32 As of May, 2025, the cairn is in process of being restored.

here. It's worth doing some research, picking up some reading material to get you through the dicey weather before touring around this really interesting piece of historical ground. And then visit or revisit some of these marvellous places.

Elder wisdom and storytelling

August 4, 2022

> "The small rural churches are closing, the schools are being consolidated, and so the only things left that represent the community are the halls."

A good friend delivered the above statement not long ago. The halls are taking the place of what used to happen in neighbourhoods in those churches and school gyms years ago.

The fact that Annapolis County believes in this fact is a blessing to all our neighbourhoods. The County has supported getting roofs and stairs fixed, paint jobs done and even some events over the years. These halls are the glue that keep rural folks together for wedding and funeral receptions, children's birthday parties, family reunions, Christmas potlucks, book sales, and card parties.

And one other important thing happens in these halls: storytelling. Most of the people who volunteer are in the elder category. They have knowledge of the history of the community and the families who have lived here. They know who has gone off to university. They remember who married whom. They remember storms that kept the power down for days. They know about the time on the Annapolis River before the tidal power plant went in and what the traffic was like on the river. Some even worked on that power plant project.

Folks remember when Ernest Buckler lived just down the road and wrote all those books and became famous.

They remember when the hall was something else—a one-room school or a Temperance Hall. They remember when just about everyone worked at the "elastic plant"—Britex. And they know that the dentist down the road bought the old plant and there have been conversations about what he's going to do with it.

I have figured out what our calling is when we are closer to the end than the beginning. It's our job to tell the stories of our communities, and our friends and our relatives. These are stories that we can hand down to the next generation.

That next generation will remember those stories when they reach a "certain age" and tell them to the next bunch, and so on.

Storytelling is an important way to remember friends and the good things that happen in the places where we live.

Houses tell stories

March 16, 2023

It was the lilacs, with their thick gnarly trunks and suckers coming up everywhere outside the front door, that gave away the age of the house when we looked at it, all those years ago. Living in a house with lots of age gives only some of its stories away no matter how much is required to live in it in today's world.

While we have moved on, our story has become part of that house now and there are new chapters being written.

Houses tell stories of the people who lived there. While there aren't exactly ghosts (some may disagree here), it seems sometimes that there are shadows of fun times and sad times. There are the faint smells of cooking dinner for a special occasion and there are smells of the wood-stove keeping the kitchen warm while baking bread all those years ago.

When we talk about built heritage, that is what we mean. Buildings that belong to a time long ago when a family lived there. Or the time when a widower farmer lived by himself, looking after the cows and the market garden well after he was blind. And there was a rope taking him out to the garden that needed weeding.

And built heritage says that there will be spring bulbs coming up in places you didn't know about until spring came along and there are snowdrops by the front steps and the irises are greening up and that patch of crocuses starts blooming in amongst the grass.

Some heritage houses and properties even have family cemeteries, with a few markers of various sizes depending on the wealth of the family at the time.

In the countryside, these homes and barns seem to be lasting much longer than those in the cities. What a shame those city homes are being toppled to make way for rather featureless apartment blocks. Those new places don't feel like homes to me. They feel like waystations from a family home to the next station in life and onwards towards a home that will last and share its family stories with the next generation.

The people in Nova Scotia are being quite firm in their call for better built-heritage protections. The Heritage Trust of Nova Scotia is asking that we tell our MLAs what built heritage means to us. Their website has some guidance on actions we can take.

By the way, did you know that the present Nova Scotia Property Act "allows owners of municipally registered heritage buildings to demolish them after a three-year waiting period, a provision that exists nowhere else in Canada"? This is the kind of information you can find on the Trust's site.

People come to this part of our country to see where we started. It is up to us to keep this history "book" intact for the next generations.

Apples

October 12, 2023

For the past couple of weeks we have been going through a large of number books that we put in boxes very carefully after our move to town. There are a lot of books, believe me.

The sorting has come down to a number of different categories:

keepers
recyclers
giving to friends
giving to the Annapolis Royal Friends of the Library (ARFoL).

The ARFoL books get separated into fiction and non-fiction.

And while all the above might seem like housekeeping stuff (it is), books have a way of making you think of things or remember things, or remember people.

One book went to the top of my pile of keepers: *Valley Gold* by Anne Hutten. It was first published in 1981 and is the history of the apple industry (it's hard to use the word "industry" when it comes to growing things) in the Annapolis Valley.

My copy has a few scribbles in it so I'm not sure if it came from one of those boxes of books Blain Henshaw used to sell at his auctions at the Royal Canadian Legion in Annapolis Royal, or whether it came from a friend.

As this is the time of year when apple pickers are needed and the new crops are coming to our stores, and last weekend was Thanksgiving, I thought I'd talk about apples this week.

Golden apples stories are many in Greek mythology. My favourite is the one in which the Golden Apples in the Garden of Hesperides were a wedding gift to Hera from Gaia and were protected by a great serpent called Ladon. The Apples, as well as the rest of the life in the Garden, were tended by the Hesperides, minor earth goddesses or nymphs and daughters of the Titan, Atlas. Another part of the story involves Hercules and his 11th labour. I will leave that tale for you to look up.

We move forward from those olden Greek days to 1698 in this part of the world, when a French census records some 1,584 apple trees growing in the gardens of 54 families at Port Royal, according to Ms. Hutten. And so the fruit trees have been planted and cared for here in this valley for 325 years.

During those years, many different varieties have been developed. The French certainly knew about grafting and growing different kinds of apples and brought that skill with them when they settled on the banks of the *rivière Dauphin*.

The history of the orchards is long in this part of North America. It is woven into the history of the people who have lived here since 1604. It is a happy story in some ways and a sad story in others, about the different kinds of Nova Scotia apples that became famous around the world, the ancient orchards that hikers come across when they journey through the forests here, and the stories of ancient trees that were cut down when the apple "industry" fortunes went through the floor after World War II.

Those orchards gave fruit to Europe every year in boatloads of barrels that went from small docks all along the Annapolis River, from the tidewater of Bridgetown to Annapolis Royal, and then across the sea to be relished in Britain.

And there were the apple drier production buildings which seemed to catch fire on a regular basis.

There are still old barns with barrel staves and hoops and boxes of accounting books in this part of the Valley. There were people in 1981 who knew all the stories about the orchards and where those apples went each year. Ms. Hutten spoke to many of them.

The last home we lived in had a field out back that showed where an orchard had been with the rows of slightly raised beds. I understand the owner of that orchard cut those trees down when an edict came out that all orchards should be sprayed to prevent diseases and insects from spreading throughout this lucrative crop.

I do not know whether this story is true or if it was a form of protest by the farmer, but for sure the orchard is not there anymore.

Anne Crossman's

Living in the County

For many years, I have thought of myself as an urban person, a denizen of big cities. However, as I look back, it seems I have lived most of my life in small towns and rural areas around the country. It seems to suit me, knowing my neighbours and caring about issues that rural folks have.

I even ran for a seat on the Annapolis County Council once. While I didn't win, it was fascinating to meet all those people while I was campaigning.

Anne Crossman's

Anger: yesterday, today and tomorrow

December 17, 2020

While "anger" isn't new and particular to this time, there certainly seems to be a lot of it going around. It would be easy to start around 2015, when the presidential campaign ramped up in the U.S. However, I feel quite certain it's been around for a long time before that. Remember the 1960s and the demonstrations against the Vietnam War? I certainly do. I was one of the marchers back then, in Halifax.

However, we are now dealing with this era of anger. There was some kind of thunder and black clouds unleashed in 2016 when the Donald Trump was elected President for the first time. The doors were flung open and all those people who felt they were hard done by came out in droves, faces contorted with rage, and expressed their fury with fists and spittle flying into TV cameras. Some of that tumult was understandable.

It happened in our own country as well. First Nations which had long-held grievances came out of the shadows. Black people in Canada have made their voices heard—quite rightly.

And it happened here in our own small corner of the world, in Annapolis County. There are the Extinction Rebellion people, who are very "angry" about the spraying and clear-cutting of Nova Scotian forests. There were some very "angry" people who started a group here a few years ago and were angry about a contract awarded to a company outside of the county to supply pharmacological supplies to (what was then) Mountain Lea Lodge in Bridgetown. Then they found a few other things to be angry about—decisions about garbage, decisions about internet connectivity and decisions about an international school project.

I looked for the synonyms for the word "Anger" and "Angry" and here is what I found –

Nouns: annoyance, vexation, exasperation, irritation, irritability, indignation, pique, displeasure, resentment, rage, fury, wrath.
Verbs: annoy, irritate, exasperate, irk, vex, put out, provoke, pique, gall, displease, enrage, incense, infuriate, madden, inflame.

I would not pretend that I have not been any of those Nouns. Nor would I let you think that I have not expressed any of those Verbs. I have certainly had my share of rants and rages.

Since the onset of COVID-19 in March, 2020, I have noticed that the temperature has risen considerably on my Facebook feed. I have said some things that I should not have, I'm sure. There has been "disrespect" along with some anger in the feed as well.

But here's my point, it's one thing to be angry about a situation or with someone. It's another to bash about willy-nilly with name-calling and uninformed opinions. Reading up on a subject helps, asking questions of those who know the facts helps, and taking a deep breath and thinking about the person you are about to unleash the wrath of (pick a god) upon helps as well.

We live in a beautiful part of this blue orb in the universe. We are here for a short time in the grand scheme of things.

Those things will change. We will grow, we want everyone here to do the best they can and be the best they can. This disease will go away or be controllable at some point—with luck, sometime next year. Let's hang on and be kind.

And my absolute favourite synonym for "anger" is *ebullition*, as in an "ebullition of fervour."

Christmas presents

January 7, 2021

"So what did you get for Christmas?" echoed throughout the land, as it has done for many years, at least as long as I can remember.

You have to understand that I live in a rather advanced-age household. All three of us can be classed as seniors, old folks or elders (my preferred appellation). I have mentioned Sally, the black Lab, before. She is up there in age, too, with her whitening face.

So this past Christmas was the most subdued business that I can remember. We managed a few decorations. We had a roast chicken, stuffing and the trimmings and plum pudding on the day. But we were only three, counting the dog.

Back to the prezzies. We went electronic this year. We have new cell phones, a new tablet, a big new monitor and something called a Raspberry Pi (not a spelling error). The week between Christmas Day and New Year's Day was spent eating leftovers for a few days and figuring out the gizmos.

The conversations went something like this:

> "How do I turn off those annoying doodle-ee-dos? It's driving me crazy!"
> "You go to your settings and look for..."

And then there's

> "Where the heck is that thing that connects my Fitbit to my phone?"

> "I used to be able to call you, but I can't find you on this new phone!"
> "Do you have my cell number or the landline number? You have to find your contact list."
> "Where the heck is that?"

> "Oh, look, the radar on the weather thingie shows we're really going to get hammered in twenty minutes."

> "This is so complicated—it's just not intuitive."
> "Well, you have to be patient. You wanted the same new phone that I got so you could ask me how to make it work. Stay with it."

> "I can't find the Conjunction Christmas Star thingie. That app doesn't want to work or something."
> "Be patient, fiddle with the controls a bit."

And on and on until we have to upgrade again in another two years, I expect.

So let me tell you about the Raspberry Pi gizmo. It's a little pink keyboard with Linux as its OS. See? I can talk the lingo.

But in order to make it work, you have to have a monitor, right? So there it sits, this little pink thing and a huge monitor. And it can't speak out loud. So off to the computer store to get speakers because none of our three sets of variously-aged speakers can plug in to the little hole or the USB thingie. And it's not mine.

You will notice that the word "thingie" appears quite often here. I haven't the strength to learn all the new lingo, so this will just have to do.

In the meantime, I learned that I can watch a YouTube video on the TV because, who knows why or how—I hit something, possibly by mistake —and there it was, interrupting some important political ghastliness. Then I couldn't figure out how to get out of it. So I had to turn everything off and start over, or, as we like to say in this new world, reboot.

I have learned how to set up a Zoom meeting and I have participated in an MS Team meeting and I haven't messed up badly on either. I know where the mute thingie is, and all that. I am learning online-meeting etiquette and the dog has been seen by complete strangers. I have also had a peek at people's décor, artwork and libraries and, when things have slowed down a tad, been able to check out the book titles.

And so now it's your turn—what did you get for Christmas?

Authors

April 8, 2021

I am just finishing a book I might not have read if my husband had not bought it. Ern Dick, a CBC colleague of mine, wrote it about the life and times of Austin Willis: *Silver Hair, Golden Voice*[33]. Ern was the CBC archivist when I knew him, and when we moved here, there he was just down the road in Granville Ferry.

He has put together a series of interviews done just before Austin Willis died. The tales are quite candid and great fun to read—especially the bits behind the scenes of radio and television back in the day.

Related to this, I think you might get a kick out of film called *The Bush Pilot*, done in 1947 and now on YouTube[34]. You have to read Ern's book for the back-story.

---

33   Nimbus Publishing
34   youtube.com/watch?v=p_c6-H97TO0

Austin Willis and J. Frank Willis are the Maritime guys I grew up listening to and watching when I was a tad younger. I remember meeting Frank at a party in Halifax in the olden days. He actually flirted with me! Mind you, he probably flirted with every woman who was there, but....

I feel fortunate to have met a number of authors over the years. Being a friend of someone who has actually written a book or two is quite rewarding for me. I think I've mentioned a friend from long ago, Silver Donald Cameron. I worked on a TV program with him years ago and met up with him and his author wife, Marjorie Simmons, many years later. I just finished reading his last book, *Blood in the Water*.

I have also recently read old friend Steve Kimber's novel, *The Sweetness in the Lime*[35]. It is fun to see how he has woven some of his own background into a novel. I got the real sense I was reading something that Steve wrote.

Annapolis County has had its share of historians, novelists, poets, playwrights and writers over the centuries. Here is a list of those I remember. I'm sure there are others.

> Peggy Armstrong, Bob Bent, Barbara Bishop, Ernest Buckler, Linda Bent, W.A. Calnek, Joe Casey, Paul Colville, Wayne Currie, Ern Dick, Evelyn Eaton, Dianne Hankinson-LeGard, Ian Lawrence, Andrew Merkel, Barry Moody, Charlotte Perkins, Bill Percy, Denise Rice, Brenda Thompson, Kent Thompson, Raymond Weir, Dave Whitman.

We have a publishing company here, too—Moose House Publication. There is a printer in Bridgetown—Integrity Printing. And we can't forget the first Canadian play, written back in 1606 at Port-Royal by Marc Lescarbot, *Théâtre de Neptune*.

I have great admiration for those who "put pen to paper". It is a long-drawn-out process that becomes subject to the whims of the huge "realm of readership" out there. When one does hear something back, it is likely not pleasant. Every now and then, a nice remark comes in which the author gloms onto with much gratefulness.

During this Time of COVID, well over a year now, many of us are devouring written words, whether in book form or electronically, and we are ever so much in debt to those of you who write. Thanks for helping us through this.

---

35 Vagrant Press

In praise of community halls

April 15 and 22, 2021

Our local worthies held the Annual General Meeting of the Centrelea Community Hall last week. We couldn't hold this meeting in the hall itself, as it needed some repairs, so we held it in the Centrelea Baptist Church, which is right across the road.

I mention this because I am a really big fan of community halls. These places have been around for a long time here in Annapolis County, across the province and even around the world, I imagine. This is where important events took place for the people who lived in the vicinity. The halls hosted events that meant more people could get together for an occasion. Especially if they wouldn't fit in someone's kitchen or parlour.

Lunches after funerals, lunches after baptisms, birthday parties, lunches after marriages, card parties, Christmas potlucks, New Year's Eve dances – all were events worthy of sandwiches, salads, baked beans, lasagna, meatballs, ham, pies, squares, cookies, tea, juice and coffee.

Some halls were something else before they belonged to the whole community. Our hall was the school, and there are some lovely photos and scrapbook pages of it from the 1940s which exist in the community. The school was moved from the space in front of the now-defunct Britex building to its present site and in, 1992, became the community hall.

There is at least one community hall which was a Temperance Hall back in the day. And there's an IOOF (Independent Order of Odd Fellows) Hall here as well.

The hall in Round Hill was, as they say, purpose-built in 1889. The Bridgetown *Monitor*, 22 April 1891, tells of a gathering "within the handsome new hall." According to the history of Round Hill by Merle Gibson, this hall was financed by selling shares to members in the Community. The hall was used by various groups such as OddFellows, Sons of Temperance, and the Women's Institute.

The mapannapolis.ca website has descriptions of many of the county's community halls. I will include some of them here to give you an idea of their variety and the places they were built.

- **Tupperville**'s hall started in 1903 and was a Union Hall. The land was purchased from Mr. Alfred Inglis for twenty dollars.
- From the Bridgetown *Monitor* - Oct 24, 1883: The inhabitants of **South Williamston** had erected a neat comfortable Temperance Hall.
- The original deed for this building was for "The Trustees for the **Brooklyn** Public Hall for the people of Brooklyn and Clarence". The deed stated that if a trustee could no longer act as such, he was to be replaced by someone of the same religious denomination. Oral tradition says that this was the Brooklyn Union Church. The church was originally located close to the north side of the highway, next to the school. It was moved to its present location by Al Peppard [1973-1984].
- This property was originally known as "**Arlington** School Section 13". The original deed is unrecorded but in 1970 the property was turned over to the Trustees of the "Mount Rose Community Club". At that time, the deed described the property as "Being the same lands used as a school property for upwards of one hundred years".
- **Margaretsville** - This building was first used as an Orange Lodge and is now the Community Hall. This hall is used by many organizations for meetings, suppers, concerts, etc. and is situated opposite a community park.
- **Parker's Cove** - Oral tradition says that this building was built as a Methodist Church. In 1887 the trustees of the Methodist Hall, Parker's Cove purchased this lot from Milledge Apt. The property was sold to the trustees for the Parker's Cove Fundy Thread and Thimble Club in 1976. The Bayshore New Horizon's Club also meets in the hall.
- **Bridgetown North** - This hall was built in 1909-10 on land that the Annapolis County Recreation Association purchased from Stephen S. Ruggles. The Recreation Association deeded the property to the Municipality in 1959. The Municipality transferred this property to the Annapolis County Municipal Housing Corporation by resolution, not by deed. The Housing Corporation decided that it no longer had any use for the Hall, so the Municipality has decided to sell it to the Bridgetown Lions Club. The Lions' Club has since moved on, but the yellow building is still there.

- **West Dalhousie** Community Hall has served the community first as a school, then as a Church Hall, and then as a Community Hall. Of the three schools in the West Dalhousie community, this is the only one left. The other two schools burned. The Community Centre can be found on the West Dalhousie Road, halfway between the Morse Road and the Thorne Road.
- **Centrelea** - This building started out as the Temperance Hall and was located on lands that used to belong to Britex Ltd., formerly United Elastic Ltd. Herbert Rice's barn was struck by lightning and it burned. The neighbours helped dismantle the Temperance Hall and move it to this site to be used as a barn on this property. And that barn has now been converted into Stirling Downs Guesthouse & Cottage.
- **Granville Centre** - Older residents remember the present Community Hall as being the former Sons of Temperance Hall situated on land given to the Sons of Temperance by Henry Roney, a great advocate of the Sons of Temperance Organization. No one can remember when it was built.
- **Belleisle** - The building has always been a hall used for community purposes. In 1911 newspaper reports stated that a new chandelier was added and that the young folks enjoyed a dance in the hall. In 1899 Benjamin Sanborn sold the property to the "Belleisle Hall Joint Stock Co." for $40.00. It remained under that name until 1987, when it was known as the Belleisle Community Club. Now being worked on for an Acadian Centre.
- **Bridgetown** - James Hillis, who started a foundry here and was general superintendent of the Bridgetown Shipbuilding company, sold this land to the Rothsay Lodge of Freemasons, Bridgetown, for their Masonic Hall. This building is now Mama Sofia's Pizzeria.
- **Inglewood** - Records at the Provincial Archives show that the school was built in 1859. The A.F. Church Map of Annapolis County (1876) has the school on this site. The old school had also been used for holding church services. It was enlarged ca. 1905. The building ceased to be used as a school in 1942. Now [1989] it is used as a Church Hall. The "new School house" referred to in the deed in 1905 was made from the old school cut in two, moved back farther and then enlarged. This former school building was used for a time after 1942 as a community hall. Now [1989] it is owned by the Baptist Church and continues as a hall

for community activities.

- **Hampton** - Oral tradition says this building was first used as a cooper shop in 1835. The upstairs was used for a temperance hall. It was the place where the meeting was held to change the name from Chute's Cove to Hampton in 1860. The first school was held upstairs.

As the weather warms up, I expect there will be some innovative ideas for events at some of these places and probably on the grounds or as takeout meals or whatever. They used to be the heart of our communities —may they continue to be so.

If you live in a community which is fortunate to have one of these historic buildings, please consider getting involved in their fund-raising efforts—especially in this Time of COVID. You meet the nicest people, the food is always delicious and you learn a lot about where you live.

A persistent disconnect

July 17, 2021

Back in the dim past of around 2000, there existed an economic and community development agency—WVDA. There may be some folks out there that remember this community fact. WVDA's Mission Statement was:

> Building on our diverse cultural heritage, the Western Valley Development Authority (WVDA) will work with the community to create a vital, prosperous, and self-reliant region where the people have ample opportunity for a full and satisfying life. [36]

One of the WVDA projects that I remember was to have a backbone built to bring high speed internet from Halifax to Lawrencetown to serve the community college campuses along that route, and then the line would

---

36 Full disclosure: I worked there on various contracts for a few years.

go down as far as Annapolis Royal along Highway 1. Plans were to take it further to serve communities as far down as Clare.

The municipalities WVDA would bring internet connectivity to included Annapolis and Digby counties, Clare and the towns of Middleton, Bridgetown, Annapolis Royal, and Digby, and the village of Lawrencetown. All the municipalities had ownership of this technology via the WVDA agreement. The municipalities had representatives on the WVDA board. That was almost 20 years ago.

When the WVDA was shut down by the withdrawal of support by some of the municipalities, that line still belonged to them. I believe Annapolis County was the last one to withdraw from WVDA, and sold that valuable piece of technology for a song to Eastlink. And things went downhill from there.

I wanted to get connectivity when we moved here in 1999. We started with Bell dialup, had Xplornet until it drove me a tad 'round the bend whenever it snowed or the cloud cover was too thick or the little green men decided to dance in the atmosphere, went to Eastlink for a while, which wasn't great, and that's when I started saying whoever came past my door first and was reasonable, would get my business.

And along came NCS Network. That's where I am and expect to stay for the foreseeable future.

So when I saw my friend Andy Kerr's note on Facebook to his fellow Fundy Shore residents last week, I paid attention. Andy lives in Hampton, and I have his permission to quote him. Here is part of what he said,

> From the start of the Seaside implementation plan for our area, we have been second on the list for sign-ups—until yesterday. Now we have been moved to 3rd place (mid-August). I can say confidently that there have not been many regions like our little strip on the shore that has contributed to, advocated for, worked for, yelled for, advised for the installation of real high speed.

It's bad enough that cell service on The Shore has not been great over the years. Andy is right to be aggravated. People in this county have been promised reasonable internet connectivity for over 20 years. There are lots of have-nots still out there. And in spite of many confident announcements, it doesn't seem to be rolling out "on schedule".

I would not have included this subject in my grumpy remarks a few columns ago if I thought things were just rolling out smoothly. Andy knows what he's talking about.

County internet redux

September 16, 2021

One wonders aloud about the newest development in the attempt by Annapolis County to bring its residents into the 21st century with high-speed internet connectivity.

Rogers Communications has bought Cape Breton-owned Seaside Communications. This is the latest twist in an endeavour that has dogged this area for years.

To recap: The Western Valley Development Agency, with a Smart Communities grant from the federal government, had a backbone (the basic infrastructure for high-speed communications) built down the Valley. When the WVDA ended, the county ended up owning this valuable piece of infrastructure. It didn't know what to do with it, so sold it for a song to Eastlink. A number of years later, the county decided that the big companies weren't going to serve its citizens properly, so they called for bids to do the build out from the backbone. The company that won the contract didn't seem to be living up to the expectations, so the county "ended" that contract and called for a new bid. That brings us up to date.

At present, Seaside Communications has been stringing cable around. There would seem to be a few folks who now actually have high speed connectivity in the county via Seaside's efforts. There are many, many more who are not connected to this new service.

The latest piece on the county website has the month and year when different parts will be able to access the service. Those dates keep getting pushed back. I heard Warden Parish say at the August 17, 2021 Council meeting that he had met with Seaside and that the issues holding things up were permission from Nova Scotia Power to use their equipment and permission from the feds to go over streams; and that Seaside is having trouble finding people to work on the build. Warden Parish spoke to Nova Scotia Power and that issue seems to be cleared up. Now we wait on the feds. Just an aside here, why wasn't this permission sought at the beginning of the build instead of part way through?

And so, we now come to a couple of weeks or so ago, when Seaside's PR guy sent out a news release saying they had been bought by Rogers. This news could have several implications. Here are some that some to mind:

- The build could go faster as Rogers has more people to do the work.
- Rogers is huge. What kind of attention will our little piece of the universe get?
- How much clout will our county council have in that big arena?
- On the other hand, Rogers has dealt with the feds for many years now and probably knows how to get things done faster.

Who knows what will happen next? There are now three BIG players in the Nova Scotia internet saga: Rogers, Bell and Eastlink.

By the way, I wonder who went after whom in the Rogers/Seaside sale? Rogers is still waiting for the federal Competition Bureau's review (and approval) to finish their acquisition of Shaw Communications. I imagine Seaside is kind of small potatoes for Rogers to buy, in comparison.

Outside my window

September 23, 2021

My office has a window that looks out over our backyard, which has a lovely golden linden tree, a small clump of lilacs, two pear trees that give better blossoms in the spring than fruit in the fall, a very small Honeycrisp apple tree and a big green barn.

As it is still early fall (or late summer, whichever you prefer), I am able to keep the window open. I listen to what's happening in this small piece of the planet.

I hear our farm neighbour's cow "talking" to someone; I hear the farm neighbour's guinea fowl calling to their flock to make sure they haven't lost someone; there's the burrrr of a chainsaw back in the woods, probably getting wood ready for winter or hacking out some underbrush back there so the road/path doesn't close in. There is the baaaaing of the farmer neighbour's sheep calling to their young, or just checking up to see where everyone is. And there is the occasional whicker of the lovely herd of Clydesdales on the other side of us.

We check to see that everyone is all right over that fence. At least, my husband does. It saves my other neighbour an unnecessary trip up the hill.

There is the scraggly old choke cherry tree up back where the turkey vultures like to perch. There has even been the occasional bald eagle up on its bare branches.

We do hear—if the wind is right and the air is soft—the traffic noise from Highway 101, but it is not loud enough to be aggravating.

I hear the farm neighbour's tractor going somewhere, doing something farm-ish, doing important tractor work.

Somehow or other, a flock of ordinary pigeons has decided they like the bird seed that gets put out. This is to the great annoyance of the resident here. He charges out, clapping his hands and swearing a bit. They leave for a while, then fly right back to the big green barn roof.

I hear the hummingbirds at our two feeders—they have all headed south now. They squabble and zoom all summer long.

The farm neighbour's cat strolls across every now and then. We have to make sure that our 12-year-old Lab is inside when that happens, because she suddenly turns into a three-year-old racing machine when she spots the cat, and that's not good for her old heart.

Then there are the neighbourhood coyotes. Every night, their voices come in the bedroom windows sometime around midnight. It always sounds like the new kids yelling for their late-night dining providers, who are probably out getting whatever they can for takeout dinner.

Over the years we have raised families of groundhogs, skunks, red squirrels and the usual collections of moths and butterflies, June bugs, ladybugs (both varieties) and birds. I've mentioned the "hummers", but there have also been the cardinals, the chickadees, the juncos, the sparrows, the blue jays, the mourning doves, and the red wing blackbirds. There have been the occasional visitors—hawks, starlings, the little "yellow dudes", the grackles, the pileated woodpeckers, the other two kinds of woodpeckers and the yellow-bellied sapsuckers.

In another few weeks it will be a bit too cold to have the window open, so until then I will enjoy the visual and aural films that play out there, and be very grateful.

October, really?

October 7, 2021

How can it possibly be October? Is this "time passing silently and with amazing speed-ism" affecting anyone else? It seems like those sweltering, sticky humid days were last week or something.

My July birthday came and went in a blur and NOT the party I had wanted, for the second year in a row. That month joined all the others in the great gray fog of the Time of COVID. It didn't seem to matter that things of import happened—they all got lumped together.

September ended in a blaze of orange. I will remember that for a long time. When I think back to the early 1960s, I knew nothing of the Indigenous history of Nova Scotia until a Sunday drive from the South Shore to The Habitation told me a story. Maybe that's what sparked an interest: when I learned about Membertou.

I also remember the first time I went North to Yellowknife and learned about a whole new (to me) story about the first peoples of this part of the world. I had no idea. Nothing in my past linked me to that part of the country and its citizens.

This month started off with Treaty Day in Nova Scotia. A fitting time to remember that we are all treaty people. Those documents signed all those years ago with the original people of this land are vital and they must be honoured even today.

And October is the birthday month of my mother, who is gone now. She was more patient with me than I deserved, but we finally got to understand each other. And it is the birth-month of my dear sister-in-law, of whom I am most fond.

October is the month in 1956 when my family and I returned from overseas after three years away. We sailed up the St. Lawrence River to Montreal and the glorious colours on both sides of the ship were breathtaking. I saw a man weep seeing those colours—mostly the red maple leaves welcoming their folks home.

This is the month of Thanksgiving for the harvest time. The last of the food for both humans and animals is both savoured and preserved for the coming Time of Whiteness.

There were deaths over these past months—too many. There were new views to see. There were letters of wonderment and condolences. There were caring thoughts sent out to many from my place here. I received many caring thoughts over this Time of COVID for various important milestones in my life.

But they all seem to be tangled in a basket like knitting gone awry or an unfinished sweater or a cross-stitch piece partially done. I remember the colours, but it's possible the patterns have disappeared.

This wretched Time of COVID has robbed some of their reason and there are those terrible suffering stories of people around the world who have fallen to this virus.

And so we are now in another October. Download your record of vaccination onto your cell phone, or print it off, as you may need it. There's a hard time coming yet again, my friends.

The road

October 21, 2021

A good friend of mine is a writer, Paul Colville. He lives on Delusion Road in Moshers Corner, Annapolis County. A while ago, he sent me a piece about Highway 101. I asked him if I could use it because it was a nice piece of local history and I like Paul's writing. Here it is.

Highway 101 South Committee
By Paul Colville

Late in 1978, John Buchanan's Progressive Conservatives won the Nova Scotia provincial election and formed a majority government. A final decision on the exact route of the new 101 Highway was expected soon. The question had been discussed for years. Should the new highway proceed on the 'North Route', down the floor of the Annapolis Valley, or would public pressure prevail and force the Department of Highways to have the road cross the Annapolis River in Kings County and follow the 'South (Mountain) Route' to the Bear River Bridge? Peter Nicholson, the long-time MLA for Annapolis West and Minster of Finance, as well as the Deputy Premier in the defeated Gerald Regan Liberal government, had for years insisted that the route run 'South' in spite of the Provincial Highway Department's preference. As a result of the election, the question as to which route to take was back on the table.

"Well, we are back to square one, by the look of things," complained my friend Terry Crowe. Terry and I became friends shortly after he arrived in the Valley in 1973. He was hired as Planning Director for the Annapolis County District Planning Commission (ACDPC). "We will have to wait and see what Gerry Sheehy and the new Tory government decides."

"You mean, 'Doctor' Gerry Sheehy. He's my veterinarian, you know. And now he has been appointed Minister of Agriculture. Surely he won't go against the farmers, who are afraid to lose land, and the Federation of Agriculture," I said, trying to ease Terry's mind.

"I don't know, Paul. This fight is not over yet."

"There's just no way Gerry Sheehy is going to side with the merchants and run the highway down the Valley floor. We'll lose over three hundred acres of prime farm land. The Women's Institute will cook his goose."

"I'm not so sure. There are far more voters in the towns than the scattered farmers around Annapolis County. And another thing," continued Terry. "I've heard that Premier Buchanan has a financial interest in the Mid-Valley Motel and wants an exit off the highway just to the west of Middleton.

"You know, about two years ago, I was at a meeting with the Department of Highways and the 101 South Committee when the citizens group asked to see the map for the North route," he recalled. "Can you believe that the Highways Department simply gave them a flat NO? They said the route had already been planned and the decisions were made. That kind of attitude just made matters worse and the 101 South people really began to organize. A public meeting was called in Annapolis Royal and I was invited to attend. I presented one of the original maps from the Highways Department showing the North route crossing a causeway to be built at the mouth of the Annapolis River, with a large 'spaghetti-like' loop of an interchange that would cut the town in half."

"No way," I said, anxious to hear what happened next.

"At first, there was just silence. And then people started to laugh. There were seventy or eighty people in the room and the place just broke up into laughter. Then reality settled in and the mood turned to anger. They could not believe that Highways was so callous—so stupid as to propose a plan that would split the historic town of Annapolis in two."

The 101 South people began to organize public meetings all over Annapolis County and a list of three goals was agreed on. It took about a year and a half of meetings, behind-the-scenes negotiating and widespread discussions in all of the county newspapers until finally a meeting with the Minister of Highways was arranged in Halifax. All the radio and television stations were there when the 101 South Committee presented its three demands:

- Get the highway up on to the South Mountain as soon as possible.
- Ensure that the highway does not split up the town of Annapolis Royal.
- Change how decisions on highway routes are made to include public consultation.

In the meantime, Terry and his staff designed a crossing over the river just to the east of the Town of Bridgetown. This would get the highway up on the South Mountain without interfering with either Bridgetown or Annapolis Royal, and yet be close enough to satisfy the merchants.

On January 12, 1979 Dr. Sheehy announced that the 101 Highway would follow the 'North' route and connect all the Valley towns just as the railroad did when it was built about one hundred years earlier. The announcement finally put an end to most of the squabbling and disagreement among the two different factions that had fought to influence the government's decision. The citizen-action group, Highway 101 South Committee, claimed a partial victory, while the merchants and towns folk backing the 'North' alignment breathed a sigh of relief.

Terry Crowe's compromise suggestion of crossing the river before Bridgetown was successful in preserving the historic towns of Bridgetown and Annapolis Royal. A traveller driving west on the 101 Highway can't help but notice how the road takes a very sharp turn to the south and crosses the Valley floor before it climbs up on to the South Mountain. Those of us who can remember the battle with the Highways Department can almost see—in our mind's eye—the warriors of the Highway 101 South Committee standing guard and directing traffic away from town.

The citizens finally forced governments to listen to the people before it made decisions affecting their towns. It is now government policy to seek citizen participation in decision-making, especially when choosing the routes for a highway right of way.

Thanks for reminding us, Paul, how things get done when citizens' common sense kicks in.

A year gone by

November 4, 2021

This column marks the end of one year scribbling away for the AV *Register*. Who knew I could find enough to write about 52 thoughts, meanderings, small explosions, and wonderings?

As I think back over this Year of COVID, I wonder how we will think of this in the years to come. There will be children who will remember the time they went to school at the kitchen table and then wore masks to real school. And there will be weddings which weren't exactly what the brides had in mind but were glad they did it. There will be babies born during this time as well.

There will the sadness of loss, too. Not all of the loss will have been due to COVID-19, but there was loss for sure.

This also marks the end of the first year of the now-not-so-new Annapolis County Council. The Nova Scotia Court gave the county $750 for expenses to do with that Farren/County legal matter over Upper Clements

Park. That session isn't over yet.

The other county legal matter had to do with the waste transfer station in West Paradise. The county had to pay a fine of $100, give $10,000 to a local environmental group (they will be lining up at the door) and remediate the property within two years and/or find a sensitive use (deemed so by the Department of Environment) for the property which the county owns.

I would like to know what positive project(s) this council has in mind. I haven't heard a whisper. There are only three more years to go, and it takes planning and foresight to make things happen.

The bigger political picture was not too surprising. The Liberals stayed about the same in Ottawa. The issues are the same and some are more pressing than others—think climate crisis and the pandemic. The Tories here in Nova Scotia don't seem to be screaming maniacs. Less sane is the ridiculous non-voting on bills of gargantuan proportions that aren't getting passed for one reason or another in the Country to the South.

Restaurants and shops have found ways to deal with the pandemic in safe mode, and have been really glad that local folks are shopping locally.

The weather here in the county has been quite wonderful. Spring arrived with the right amount of sun and rain. Summer was a tad humid for me, but all the fruiting trees and bushes loved every minute of it. There were apples and pears and all the succulent berries you can name in abundance this year.

And, last but not least, I am still not able to see my far-flung family. It would involve flying to see them or they would have to get here to see us. I am saving up all my birthday parties for a lollapalooza. It had better happen soon—I might just run out of time. Maybe next year.

I'm sure there are other notables that belong here, but such is the way of pandemics. They kind of freeze your brain, and close and lock the file drawers of memory for eternity. There were significant things I may never remember. However, I will "build" a new file cabinet and start stowing memories away as they happen.

I'd like to end by thanking all you readers out there who have kept in touch through all the various electronic means. You lift my heart.

A night at the theatre

December 2, 2021

I believe I know what the Renaissance period must have been like after the Black Death in the 1300s. I think I actually experienced it a couple of weeks ago, at Annapolis Royal's King's Theatre. I was amongst my fellow human beings, laughing and applauding and thoroughly enjoying ourselves (albeit masked, vaccinations required, and ID'd).

I don't think I realized how much this pandemic had affected me. I really don't go out very much, that's true. I am fortunate to have someone in my household (we are two and a dog) who braves the grocery and drug stores when required.

I came out of that theatre just buzzing! I couldn't stop talking to my neighbour who drove me home. I was still excited when I walked through my door.

It was kind of like Christmas, New Year's Eve, a birthday, and July 1st for me. I didn't even feel embarrassed by my buoyancy. It was just lovely to have that kind of feeling again.

The plays written by Wayne Currie were delightful. There was fun, silliness, introspection, nostalgia, strangeness and "what the heck was that?" on that stage.

And there were people I know on the stage and behind the scenes. I am always in awe of people who will put themselves out there to be looked at intensely and who will memorize the lines and make us feel something. When they are friends and neighbours, that just makes it that much more fun.

I am quite sure my reactions have been heightened by this damned virus. That's okay. Those reactions have been missing in my life for 625, days just like in everyone else's life. That's 1 year, 8 months and 15 days.

There have been milestones happening during this recent past. Friends have passed away. Acquaintances have moved or had babies. I have gone to meetings of small groups, learned how to Zoom and Teams, learned how to use Messenger, shared emails, made phone calls, watched

Netflix movies, shared photos of long ago and far away, and culled books for the Friends of the Library in Annapolis Royal.

We've had time to go back over old memories that seem to have surfaced as we've had time to contemplate and cogitate.

But that feeling coming home from that little theatre in Annapolis Royal will carry me for quite a while. It was just glorious and still seems to be hanging on.

May a real Renaissance begin. The arts and cultural communities apparently flourished after that 1300s plague. May we all hope that an upwelling of desire to deal with the causes of our present climate crisis will begin—soon, very soon.

Still going strong

January 20, 2022

I do know a thing or two about people over the age of, let's say, 70. An extensive study in the U.S.[37] found that the most productive age in human life is between 60 to 70 years of age. And the second most productive stage for a human being is from 70 to 80 years of age.

When I was much younger, 70 seemed to be quite a long time to have lived. And then, suddenly, I was 70. As I looked back over my life and wondered if I was worth the oxygen, I finally decided that I hadn't done too badly. As far as careers go, I've actually had quite a few. That doesn't happen to everyone.

I know quite a few over-70 people who are still going strong. They are those volunteers who make all kinds of organizations and events run. They can't help themselves; it seems. They just have to be in there making sure that the hall continues to operate or that the turkey dinner gets served at Christmas or that chowder at the church gets made and served on Lenten Fridays.

There are retired teachers who are asked to substitute teach. There are retirees who run for municipal council, provincial government, and

---

37   Published in the *New England Journal of Medicine* in 2018.

federal government positions—a sometimes-thankless job, if ever there was one.

This over-70 crowd also starts new businesses—sometimes out of need for income, but also out of need to be "doing something". I know of mining executives, clean energy people, artists and writers who are over 70 and got into a new business after retirement from a position they held for 40-odd years.

Nova Scotia, apparently, is the province with the highest proportion of "seniors", and I believe we could say we also have one of the most active and vibrant group of senior citizens in the country. Our older people know a thing or two and are willing to share their talents, the wisdom they have gained over the years, and their knowledge with anyone who is willing to listen.

I believe that the Annapolis Drama group is made up of mostly over-70 people. And just look at what they have done over the years. The same is true for the *plein air* painter folks who regularly turn up at the Paint the Town event each summer in Annapolis Royal—I believe many of them are over 70.

As for authors, I have just read about a man who is now 87 and has published his 14th book on sports in the Annapolis Valley. Now that is re-markable.

There are those retired folks on the Eastern Shore who operate a community radio station. They had already put in many years in the radio/TV business.

I certainly count myself among this group. I am still learning, but I'm having a whale of a time these days, even though I am shut in and lucky enough to have friends who still answer their phones when they read who it is in that little window.

A tough ask from Nova Scotia Power

February 3, 2022

Once upon a time, there was the Nova Scotia Power Commission. Then there was the Nova Scotia Light and Power Ltd. The Liberal government of Gerald Regan took over the Nova Scotia Light and Power Ltd. That was away back in 1971.

In 1992, the Progressive Conservative government of Donald Cameron privatized Nova Scotia Power. There were 65 million common shares put on the market at $10 a share. Nova Scotians were offered a special deal whereby they could buy on an instalment plan with 60 per cent down and the rest paid within the year. Despite the good deal for Nova Scotians, 75 per cent of the shares were bought by out-of-province investors.

The above information came from a 2011 book by Richard Starr called *Power Failure?* It gives a view to the history of power in Nova Scotia since 1720. There is information on the coal industry, and on the oil and gas industry as well. The news is not good. As a matter of fact, it is a rather dreadful litany of governments and greed and mismanagement for over 300 years.

And so we come to today. The new version of Nova Scotia Power Inc. is owned by Emera Inc. Emera owns six other companies in Canada and the United States:

- Tampa Electric (Florida)
- Peoples Gas (Florida)
- Emera Caribbean (parent company of Grand Bahama Power Company and Barbados Light & Power, a majority shareholder in Dominica Electricity Services Ltd., and an investor in St. Lucia Electricity Services Ltd)
- Emera Newfoundland & Labrador (owns 100% of NSP Maritime Link Inc.)
- Emera New Brunswick (transmits natural gas through the Brunswick Pipeline)
- New Mexico Gas Co. (maintains 12,000 miles of natural gas pipeline)

The latest hullabaloo is Nova Scotia Power's application to the Nova Scotia Utilities and Review Board to hike rates and do some other tweaks to some of their rates. So let's take a look at what NSP wants.

1. Raise the rates on residential properties.
2. Raise the rates on commercial properties.
3. Put a "system access charge" on those people who put solar panels on their properties to save money and the environment. But if they already have those panels and are feeding back to the grid,

there is a moratorium of 25 years.

4. A storm rider of up to 2% on the years that have severe storms.
5. Charge ratepayers for energy saving programs that exceed $40 million per year.
6. Charge ratepayers $53 million in deferred fuel costs.
7. Create a "decolonization deferral account".
8. Maintain its 9% rate of return.

And don't forget that NSP wants to have ratepayers pay for the decommissioning of the Tidal Power Plant in Annapolis Royal.

Oh, and by the way, NSP gets all the carbon credits for those 4,100 customers who were able to put solar panels on their property and even sell power back to the grid.

The storm rider business is money for them. With climate change, our storms are more frequent and more severe.

What the heck is a "decarbonization deferral account"?

All of a sudden, NSP has discovered that burning coal is contributing to the climate crisis. They have known about this connection for at least 40 years. Now that the various governments are getting on board the climate change bandwagon, NSP wants its ratepayers to pay for it dragging its feet. And it wants to still make a profit for its parent company Emera, which is busy buying and selling energy companies.

I think NSP is going to get the small hello, as they say. And this was not a very good time to make this ask. The populace is angry. It is angry about the COVID-19 restrictions, it is angry that it can't go to restaurants, it is angry about the flip-flopping on schools, it is angry, angry, angry. And it's January and we have just had the third humongous storm. Two of them did damage to our power system and people had to make like pioneers for quite a few hours.

The anger momentum is growing on social media and the emails lists about all this.

NSP may get a few things, but I don't think the atmosphere around consumer patience is in a giving mode.

Remember the internet?

March 10, 2022

A long, long time ago, the World Wide Web was born. I was alive when this miracle of communication happened.

And then the internet became available to lots of regular folks like you and me. Except it wasn't available to all of the folks here in Annapolis County.

Apparently, other rural areas across this Big Land weren't among the privileged to have internet service, either. So the folks in Ottawa thought it would be a good idea to give some money to provinces and municipalities to see that EVERYONE who wanted internet service could get that service—for a fee, of course.

The previous Annapolis County Council decided the fastest/best way to get this now really important service to the constituents was to own the fibre that would deliver it, but it had to be built first. The first attempt ran into problems—I'm not saying anything more about that part.

The second attempt has been as "slow as molasses in January".

I do have to say that I have good service here in Centrelea and am eternally grateful. Otherwise, I'd be sending my columns off to the *Annapolis Valley Register* by carrier pigeon.

Then there was the Request for Proposals to sell the now-partially-built fibre, issued on October 4th last year. The apparent reasoning was that the County should not be in business. But we didn't hear that discussion, because it was *in camera*.

We now come to the present. Have we heard anything? Crickets!

Our duly-elected Council really needs to let its bosses know what's going on. Is the fibre being sold? Are there conditions on the sale? Who won the bid? Is it a reputable company that cares about its customers? Is there a connection deadline for all of those people who signed up to get their service? I really think they sometimes forget that we hired them. People are just plain fed up with this schmozzle.

I mentioned a couple of weeks ago that people are angry. They are angry for all kinds of other reasons, too, which are very obvious. This Council needs to get on with this.

We are waiting out here.

PS – I see the CAO's report to the Committee of the Whole meeting this past Tuesday says that he had "Various communications with staff, legal representatives and proponent regarding potential sale of Internet". That's pretty informative.

Visitors!

June 21, 2022

I wonder how complicated it is to go on the CAT ferry from Yarmouth to Bar Harbour, Maine and back without taking a car. Do you have to get off the ferry at the other end? Do you need a passport? Can you buy a return ticket and just stay on board?

I think I'd like to do that this summer. It would be like a mini cruise without pools and slides and all those other things that seem to be floating on the seas again. I'll be checking into that this week.

Speaking of the CAT, I understand there are Americans, real ones with vehicles with their license plates saying where they are from, on land here in Nova Scotia. A convoy of RVs, complete with attached cars, was also seen the other day on a Nova Scotia highway. That's pretty exciting on a couple of fronts. First, it means that the ferry is actually running and, second, that the tourists are starting to trickle in.

There are businesses that are thirsty for them. I was talking to one business person in Annapolis Royal a week ago who was very worried that the visitors didn't seem to be arriving in numbers. It's nearly the end of June and there should be more folks walking at Fort Anne or having lunch at one of the eateries or getting an ice cream cone.

I think there is still a fair amount of caution in the land. It's almost like if we start acting like there is absolutely no pandemic, we get a tad nervous. I know I feel like I have been hibernating for all this time. I find myself going out a bit more, talking to real faces more and making dates for lunch more.

As a friend pointed out, the restrictions have only been lifted here a few weeks ago. People are carrying their masks in their pockets or wearing them tucked under their chin in case a situation arises where it is the cautious thing to do—pull up the mask over the nose and smile mightily with your eyes.

The weather has been pretty nice these past few weeks and that encourages outdoor gatherings where there is lots of fresh air and the trees are green beyond belief and the Rhodies are blooming. There is lots to see and do in the month of June here in Nova Scotia.

And not to get too excited, but I saw one of those big tour buses in Annapolis Royal. When was the last time you saw one of those?

RVing for seniors

August 25, 2022

A number of years ago, I was flabbergasted to learn that seniors were selling their brick-and-mortar places and heading off into the wide blue yonder in recreational vehicles (RVs). I don't just mean a few retired people, I mean a whole big bunch of elders were on the road again, and are still on the road.

They live all over the place. Some have regular parks where they rent space for certain periods of the year. And some roam around as the spirit moves them.

I must admit I saw this as an American phenomenon. Not so. Canadians are doing it, too. And they set up their RVs in parks for the winter, too. In Canada. In the Winter.

The Canadian Camping and RV Council says there are at least 50,000 full-time Canadian RVers who normally spend winters in the U.S. So some don't spend winters here.

A friend told me recently about another adventure these folks like to visit—eateries. So there is a list of eateries that welcome RVs. You join (pay money) and you can drive across the country and set up in the restaurant/pub backyard and someone else does the cooking for you for a change. I read that there is a limit of 5 RVs per place per night. The web-site I was looking at is Terego.ca.

The other thing I learned is that there is one of those eatery spots right here at Lunn's Mill Beer Co. I certainly know them as a great place for snacking and eating, and the fact that they are just down the road helps, too. I've had many a delicious meeting there.

What a great idea, though. You roam across the country, stopping at interesting restaurants/pubs, and see all the local touristy places.

Before I get too excited about this as my next adventure, you really have to be serious about this life on the road. It can be a tad expensive depending on what features you'd like to have in the rolling abode. There are a few RV dealers in Nova Scotia—check them out before you go all Jack Kerouac.

I was rather partial to the really, really big motorhome numbers—the kind you can have a party in when you get wherever you are going. Price does become a factor there. Plus, and this is big plus, you have to know how to drive those beasts. And you have to drive them at a speed that doesn't annoy all the locals who are trying to get to the grocery store or the dentist.

Although I once had a hankering, I admit it, to live in a mobile wander-ing machine, I suspect those days are long gone. I did have a good time this week, though, looking at all the models and places where I could stay for a few weeks and take in the local atmosphere. And especially stay next to a really good eatery.

Health and power

October 13, 2022

Two pressing issues have people fretting these days. I do not mean to make light of either one, as they both deal with people's well-being.

The first one is the new model being tried at a few of the health centres to take over from the "what used to be called" emergency depart-ments.

I went to one of the information meetings the other week in Annapolis

Royal. The time for questions from the floor was limited, for sure. I have much sympathy for those who do not have a family doctor. I am fortunate to have been "grandfathered in" to the Collaborative Practice in Annapolis Royal. I have had to go to Emerg a few times. I have had to find one that was open. I have not had any issues with the system.

However, I did not go to Emerg with a hangnail or a scratch or a small ache or pain. I went when I believed it was serious. I have the distinct feeling that some people don't do that. The list of the most calls to Emerg started with prescriptions followed by UTIs (urinary tract infections). And here are some other small things that people went to Emerg with: mild headaches, earaches, minor infections, skin and eye irritations.

If you don't have a doctor, who do you call? 811 is a good starter for things like these. I know that in the "olden days" you could just call up your GP (general practitioner) and get an over-the-phone "There, there, it will be alright", "take two Aspirin and call me in the morning". Those days are long gone.

Until we support the graduation of more family doctors from the medical schools, the situation will continue. Until we have a two-year rural service program for forgiveness of part of graduates' tuition debt, the situation will continue. Until we make it less onerous (red tape, etc.) for immigrant doctors to practice here, the situation will continue.

I will pay close attention to how this new Urgent Treatment Centre works and listen when an assessment is done. In the meantime, I will call 911 if I believe it is a real emergency and have a medical professional tell me so, and follow their instructions.

The next issue is becoming increasingly vexatious: Nova Scotia Power. I understand people in the northeastern part of the province have been really fed up with the length of time it's taking to get their power up and running after Hurricane Fiona roared through and wrecked a lot of power lines.

Nova Scotia Power would like everyone to cut back their trees, so they don't fall on the power cables. Apparently, 41% of European power lines between 1 kilovolt and 100 kilovolts lie underground, according to the Europacable industry group. You heard that right: 41%, close to half.

I understand that Europe is more densely populated. I also understand that underground cables in Europe are placed in a trench while North American ones (few and far between) are placed in a piping system. I also understand that some municipalities require any new housing development have the cabling underground. I wonder if any of our Nova Scotian municipalities have such a requirement?

As we know, storms are becoming stronger. The seas are battering coastlines. The oceans are rising.

We really need to force the power companies to reinvest some of their profits into making sure the food in the freezer doesn't spoil and go to the compost heap and that the lights stay on so people can cook a meal, have a shower and have drinking water. All over the province.

Both these pressing issues are critical to the general populace. Dealing with these issues is why we elect governments. Those governments are meant to solve problems for the greater good. Although the Urgent Treatment Centre idea is at least being tried out as a solution, we'll see how it works. The issues with Nova Scotia Power and its parent company, Emera, don't seem to be going away and I haven't heard them offering solutions to their issues other than "give me money".

On the move again

October 20, 2022

I have lived in 47 houses, apartments, trailers, and tents over the years. This house in Centrelea that Alfred Messinger built in 1866 and that my husband rebuilt/renovated in 1999 has been the abode I've inhabited for the longest time in my whole life—23 years!

It's time to move...one more time.

As one ages, it seems reasonable and necessary to me that the word "downsizing" becomes much more important. That includes property. I believe leaving someone else to deal with the accumulations of stuff over a lifetime, is unfair and unkind. And I do not want to deal with selling a property and getting rid of stuff while I am trying to deal with a crisis of some sort. You know what I mean.

Now that I've got that off the agenda, here's what I am finding as I prepare to move. There are all kinds of things in the basement that bring back memories—cassette tapes, LPs, board games, books, cooking utensils, electric appliances (think George Foreman Grill), big pots and other items that won't fit in the new kitchen.

There are items on a new list coming from the barn person that I had no idea "we" owned.

There are books, books, and more books. They now fall into three categories: keepers, maybes and going to the Annapolis Royal Friends of the Library annual book sale.

Selling items is not that easy. Putting them online requires constant vigilance and back-and-forth correspondence.

Giving items away to friends is my favourite. It's easy. It's quick. Someone else gets something they want.

The lists in this house right now would fill one of those 13 3-ring binders I found in a box in the basement! There is the To Do List for changing addresses. There is the list of items for sale and their prices. There is the list of the items to give away to friends. And there are the lists for the new owners: things for sale, things for free, lists of services—snowplowing, internet provider, TV satellite service, local contractors, insurance providers. There is a list of things for the Good Will folks: clothing, linens and so on. And there are all those pictures on all the walls around here. Where are they going?

We have a great real estate agent who is helping us with advice on all kinds of things. We can do some things before the actual sale and not do others, just in case. We have a mover lined up who has been very helpful as well.

There are questions still unanswered: should we get another landline or just rely on our cell phones? Which TV and internet service should we get? Which is the most reliable?

Getting someone to do the total cleaning of this old house for the new owners just before we sign off on this place is another item on the list. Once everything has been taken away from here, I have a feeling it's going to look a little like Miss Havisham's wedding banquet room in Dickens' *Great Expectations*. Well, maybe not quite that bad, but you know what I mean.

I am also going to leave a letter telling the new people about the property and the community. It will include names of neighbours, volunteer work opportunities, pictures of the property and its history, and a "tour" of the property with its trees and gardens.

By the way, we aren't going far. Annapolis Royal will be our new location. We will be amongst friends there and will keep our friends here.

Delving into electricity

December 8, 2022

Two topics of discussion arise when the name Nova Scotia Power comes up: outages and bills. There is a certain amount of confusion and misin-formation around about this company these days. I delved into my men-tal filing cabinet to dredge up some information I have learned over the years. I have talked to people inside and outside the company for some time now in order for me to understand how it all works.

Once upon a time in Nova Scotia, each municipality owned its own electric company. Electrification first came to Nova Scotia in 1885, when the Halifax Electric Light Company inaugurated the first central electric station.

Many of these small rural companies produced their power by dam-ming rivers and streams. Some pumped water from reservoirs up to wa-ter towers and had the descent of that water go through turbines in or-der to produce power. And then some of these companies started burn-ing coal to produce power.

In 1928, Nova Scotia Light and Power Company, Limited was born. It existed until 1972, when it was taken over by the Province of Nova Sco-tia. During the time it was operating, it acquired many of the small muni-cipal power companies.

And then there is Emera. This is essentially a holding company. Emera owns seven companies in Canada, the United States and the Caribbean.

That's all the background I can fit in here without losing you, dear reader.

So Emera is in control of Nova Scotia Power and has the last word on how much the budget is going to be to upgrade the systems and so on. However, the rates we have to pay are regulated by the Nova Scotia Util-ity and Review Board. This is an independent body which regulates how much the shareholders can get and how much we customers have to pay for our power. There is a bit more to it, but we'll leave it at that.

Nova Scotia Power does not cut down trees. Municipalities have to okay that. After a wind storm or a hurricane, or a vehicle runs into your house, and if there is damage to that pipe that holds the power that goes into your house, they don't fix that. You have to hire an electrician, and the work has to pass inspection and then NSP will turn on the juice again.

And so you see, there's a lot to know about before you call NSP's outage line to start hollering about not getting power. The background gives you some idea about how long electricity companies have been around—not long in the grand scheme of things—and who to be cross at if you feel you are not being dealt with properly.

By the way, here's an interesting bit of local knowledge:

> Beckwith Electric Light Company was a small hydroelectric generating plant located on Bloody Creek, near Bridgetown...The ratepayers of Bridgetown, at a meeting called for the purpose of voting upon the purchase of the electric light system of that town on Tuesday evening [25 May, 1909], decided by a vote of 17 for and 4 against, the sum of $25,000. A vote of $20,000 was passed, and Mr. Beckwith, representing the electric light company, has declined to accept. The town is without lights, except lamps and candles.

This information is from *The Digby Courier* on June 4, 1909.

Then, in the June 18, 1909 edition of the same newspaper:

> The street lighting question, which has been perturbing the citizens of Bridgetown for so many weeks, is at last settled and the town will install its own lighting system.

Just because I'm old...

March 23, 2023

One of the phrases that keeps coming around—I know you've heard it, I know you've used it—is, "Getting old ain't for sissies." And that's true.

Possibly because we aren't sissies means that we oldsters/seniors/ elders have lived a lot. Some of us have lived even more than those younger folks can imagine.

I thought I'd give you my list of things I expect to do perfectly well until/if I get some dreaded debilitating disease.

- I am perfectly capable of paying bills. I can look after the banking myself. I do almost everything monetary-related online now. I can't remember the last time I wrote a paper cheque. I can do e-Transfers and deposit those few real cheques online.
- I keep track of my medical appointments. I keep track of all my medications—and, believe me, that's a full-time accomplishment.
- All my news comes from reliable, mainstream online news sources. I can talk about what's going on locally, provincially, nationally and internationally (in those places I'm most interested in).
- I have friends with whom I correspond regularly all over Canada, the U.S., Europe and Australia.
- Speaking of friends, I have some very special local friends who haven't given me up as a doddering fool.
- So far, I am able to make decisions affecting my well-being. I am capable of learning brand new things, too. Remember the red Bolt EUV we bought—whose name is GAIA, by the way? I have now driven it twice by myself. I haven't figured out all the icons on the big-screen TV on the dashboard yet, but I'm getting there.
- I just bought a snazzy new laptop (which weighs mightily and I have to get a bag to carry it in) and have been getting it ready to roll at the next meeting so I don't look like that old lady at the end of the table with five pounds of papers rustling them to find the right document.
- My next medical appointment will be on Zoom.

Think about the various organizations around your purview—the Legion, the fire halls, the community halls, the library boards, the historical and heritage boards, the wharf association, the town and county committees, the pool association, the community health society, and on and on. When I go to some of those meetings, the silver hair is blinding. We have many of these folks right here. And I think how lucky we are to have the experience and knowledge of the brains, hearts and souls under those silver heads.

And think about what would happen if all those older folks decided not to volunteer—just think about it, really.

Many of us elders learned much from our elders when we were younger, and still consider it an honourable thing to give back to the community now that we have the time. While the aches and pains would be good to get rid of, I'm still having a good time, and so are my friends.

A life-long passion for reading

March 30, 2023

I can't remember exactly how old I was when I started reading. I know my mother read to me. I think I read the Noddy books by Enid Blyton when I was little.

Next, each Christmas a parcel would arrive from England from my godmother, and I was on the floor in my room until New Year's Eve reading the latest adventures of The Famous Five. I kind of liked Georgie best. Enid Blyton wrote lots of those books. They lasted me until I was about 8 or 9.

Then I went through the horse book phase—many girls do, apparently. I had a friend in Ottawa named Carol whose apartment we went to after school and pretended to be various horses. There were all those Black Stallion books—Walter Farley wrote 20 of those. They were terrific. Of course, I've seen *The Black Stallion* movie with Mickey Rooney. And *Black Beauty* was a perennial favourite. There was *The Yearling*, by American writer Marjorie Rawlings.

And *The Call of the Wild* and *White Fang* by that radical, Jack London —I didn't know the radical part until many years after reading the books. *Beautiful Joe*, written by Canadian Marshall Saunders, was in my grandmother's bookcase. I think I read that one a couple of times.

As I got a bit older I read some of my mother's books, which I believe had belonged to *her* mother. I have a few of those still. I don't remember the names of all those books and have read many, many books since those early introductions into the lands and feelings of faraway places and people and imaginary creatures.

Recently, I have tried reading some political books. I am having a hard time trucking through yet another view of the guy with the really long red tie. I will be taking more time with that one, I think. I found Obama's book, *A Promised Land*, interesting.

But the ones I really like these days are about those Vikings. I'm fond of the Templars. And there's a series of books about Cadfael, a fictional Welsh Benedictine monk who lives in about 1140 in Shrewsbury, England. And there's Ken Follett and all his wonderful historical novels.

I like historical novels, it seems. One of my favourites is *Quietly My Captain Waits*, by Evelyn Eaton. She wrote this book in one of Joe Casey's cottages in Victoria Beach and it is about one of my favourite historical figures in these parts, Louise de Freneuse. I also just like saying her name out loud.

I note that I have three books on the go these days: Maggie Haberman's book on Trump (mentioned above); another Brad Thor book; and *Mrs. Dalloway*, by Virginia Woolf—a very hard slog with little punctuation and pretty wild streams of consciousness.

Books, for me, have been a place to go for many reasons. Sometimes to "get out of here." Sometimes to learn something. Sometimes to be soothed and sometimes to be moved—those "have the tissues handy" books.

My book-lover friends don't all have an electronic reader as I do. They haunt used bookstores and go to the local library. I have lived in remote parts of this country and haven't always been able to get to either of those lovely places to browse. I finally caved in, went digital, and been happily reading away on my device ever since.

Travelling adventures

April 13, 2023

We had to go on a long trip last week, from one side of Canada to the other. We have discovered that we are just like those first-time old people you used to see on planes who made you say things like, "Gawd, I hope we just stay home when we are that age!"

We started in Nova Scotia with a major sleep deficit—up at 4 a.m., driving to the Halifax airport at 7:30 a.m. to catch a 12:30 p.m. plane. We were behind the 8-ball already.

My legs don't work as well as they used to (I am baring my soul here), but I thought I could make it from the parkade down to the ticket counter—nope. I got left with the baggage about halfway down the hall while my travelling companion went whipping down to get the wheelchair. On the way back to the ticket counter there was a great horde of people who really didn't seem to want to get out of the way, so there I was hollering (with a smile, of course) "Coming through!" and "Beep, beep!" I really didn't think they moved very quickly, but we managed.

The WestJet folks treated us like royalty. We got the wheelchair to the ramp, got on the plane, and set off for Toronto.

When the pilot said we should keep our seatbelts on because there might be some turbulence, he wasn't kidding. I have flown on Twin Otters, helicopters, Beavers, float planes and a few others I can't recall the names of. This turbulence was almost a teeth-breaker.

Landing in Toronto was pretty special, too. We must have left a quarter of the rubber on the tires on that runway.

The gate for the Calgary flight was right there. We were amazed. Hardly any stopping time. I was still in the wheelchair and there was hovering by the staff so we knew that we hadn't been forgotten.

And then off to Calgary. The excitement is building, I can tell.

Eating on planes is always an adventure. But I sure don't remember dealing with the snack packaging in great detail. This time, there were gluten-free beef pepperoni sticks—I think there were four of them. The first 15 minutes were taken up by trying to start tearing the package without your jackknife (you know), the next 15 were spent trying to decide if there were germs on that packaging because, if there were, you couldn't use your teeth to open the thing up. Then there was the peeling of the plastic down the length of this gluten-free delight. It kept my travelling companion busy for ages—remember, there were four of those packages.

I won't mention the crackers in a sealed pouch or the pretzels or the gummy bear packaging, as I can hear your eyes rolling from here.

I got spun about through an airport I used to know after many trips up North, a nice young man (emphasis young) whistling me along, with my 80-year-old companion trying to keep up, carrying the carry-on stuff for miles and miles to the right gate, where I got parked.

And then I got sideswiped by a nice older man in *his* wheelchair, being pushed by his wife. He was most concerned, but his wife didn't say a thing and just kept on pushing.

I started to laugh—probably a case of sleep-deprived hysteria—and a couple of ladies across the waiting room area started to laugh. They were going to Ottawa and said that we should make sure they put me on the right plane—not theirs. It deteriorated from there.

The plane to Victoria, B.C. was a bit late leaving as a group from Rome was late getting in and, as the lady with the microphone said, "We wouldn't want them to miss Easter with family."

As we were sitting there watching everyone get to their seats with masses of bits of luggage hanging off them, I didn't see one cane. The first time we flew to Vancouver Island on business, many years ago, we chuckled and said, "Of course, we're going to Victoria, the city of the retired and the aged," which was kind of cruel, I know. What we did see was really young families with little kids and babies. We didn't hear a peep from any of them.

The washroom adventure via wheelchair in Victoria started with a traffic jam, dodging people trying to get in and then waiting for someone who needed help getting out. There was one lady with a cane who was directing traffic.

On the way out, we dodged a lady with a stroller with a whole lot of bags coming in and, as there was no room, she left. A lineup outside was waiting to get in when my daughter finally manoeuvred us out. I smiled and waved and thanked everyone.

Oh yes, in spite of all those air traveller horror stories, our checked bag arrived with us on the same plane and hardly took any time at all to reach the carousel.

I will refrain from telling you about the return trip, I promise.

Annapolis Royal shines

June 1, 2023

This past week was a whirlwind of musical intake for me and a reminder of what a remarkable place Annapolis Royal is.

First, there was a fundraiser at King's Theatre (love that place) for the restoration of the Schafner Point Lighthouse, now being called the Port Royal Lighthouse. It is in disrepair and needs fixing up. The plans are great and there seems to be quite a neighbourhood group both working and fundraising to make this Light a place to remember when light-houses mattered more than they do today on the Annapolis Basin.

There is a really good website[38] which gives some information on this lighthouse and others around the province.

Back to the musical evening. It was really, really good. Lynnea Rose opened for The Rhinestone Romeos. I have heard of the Romeos, and I know Bill MacDonald, one of its members. However, this was the first time I had heard them play. They are incredibly professional, they know their stuff, they can sing like mad, and the guitars are excellent. The audience was singing along.

Lynnea Rose did a terrific duet with Bill Mac and their voices blended superbly. It turns out that she is the granddaughter of Peggy Armstrong (1929-2019), a much-loved playwright in these parts. It was my honour to help Peggy edit *Age of Sail in Annapolis County 1760 – 1925* for a second printing. Going to visit her and making sure I was getting it right was one of the delights of doing the work.

On Sunday I went to St. George and St. Andrew's United Church to hear A Royal Consort present a very different kind of program called Let's Sing Together. There were some classical pieces, a fun piece with 10 TV program theme songs and Leon Dubinsky's **We Rise Again**. We sang that one with the choir and a wonderful soprano (whose name I didn't catch), who hit that high note with confidence and made it her own.

The Annapolis Royal Farmers and Traders Market is back at Market Square on Wednesdays and Saturdays. Bistro East is open for brekkie and lunch after its recent change of owners. Plans are being made to spruce up Market Square and to work on the last third of the Wharf.

The O'Dell House Museum, the Sinclair Inn and North Hills Museum opened this past week with enthusiastic new summer people, including a gentleman attired as a Loyalist. You will see him at the Market and at North Hills Museum. Fort Anne National Historic Site is open.

My new hometown (I am now referred to as a "townie") has come to life for another year. For a town of 567 (as of July, 2022) and occupying 1.98 square kilometres, this tiny place is really something. And it has been something for 418 years.

---

38 nslps.com/about-ns-lighthouses/lighthouse-lists?c=schafner-point-light-house

Anne Crossman's

COVID-19

When our country shut down in March of 2020, it seemed to me that all kinds of things closed but there were other events and opportunities that opened up. I did all the rather silly things like making bread again, but it became an even more neighbourly thing to do.

We were all in the same boat, trying to figure out how we were going to make our ordinary life work when businesses were trying to come up with ways to make what they offered available to their customers. We also tried to find hobbies or other stay-at-home things to do.

Anne Crossman's

Thoughts in the Time of COVID

May 13, 2021

I am an inveterate glass-half-full person. Those who know me know that I can be critical, too, but it is very easy for me to see the good in folks and things.

I see a lot more sunrises and sunsets on social media these days. I see cats (oh boy, do I see cats!) and dogs and little kiddos and wondrous works of creativity. I was wondering if people are paying a bit more attention to these joyous things than they used to—a new flower in the garden, a bee zooming in to a flower in Annapolis Royal's Historic Gardens, an old postcard of a forgotten place, a lovely old photo of someone loved taken long ago and far away, and little sayings to lift us up.

Last Sunday was Mother's Day. Even though this was an "invented" day for commercial reasons some time ago, it feels like we all need a large dose of mothering these days. I know I sure could. This virus and its rampage seem to magnify every little aggravation. There are some very frightened people around who could use a mothering hug.

We all know the drill: stay home; IF you have to go out, wear a mask; be safe; and be kind. It helps to do all these things if you are retired, have a partner to help out, own your own home, and don't have to worry too much about spending money. I can't imagine what it would be like to have a couple of kiddos at home, needing to go to work because you need the money, can't afford a babysitter, let alone day care, paying an exorbitant rent, heat, light, water, phone AND groceries. It sounds so hard, especially as this has been over a year now.

My phone calls to dear friends are getting shorter and the subject matter just gets repeated and repeated—health report; vaccine report; weather report; political stuff—local, provincial, national, US; latest book read; latest movie watched; and wouldn't it be lovely if...?

Back to the good stuff now to finish up. The red and yellow tulip bulbs, planted years ago, that I bought from the Legion via the lovely Bill Hirtle, are blooming like mad; the daffodils are out in drifts (well, small ones, but I like that phrase); the trees are greening up; the winter door was taken down; the grass has been mowed for the first time this year; the ewes and lambs have been out next door; there's a new foal in the neighbourhood; our firewood for next winter was delivered; AND the first hummingbird has been to the feeder.

Epidemics and art

May 20, 2021

I have had occasion to use our Medicare system over the past years. I am grateful for it in so many ways. I am grateful for the health centres and the hospitals. I am overwhelmed by the care I have received from the collaborative practice people at the Annapolis Health Centre: the nurses, the out-patients people, the emergency people, and the Emergency Medical Technicians (EMT)s. I have had nothing but care and competence from them all.

I have been there more than once. I like this way of doing things during the Time of COVID. There are times when a visit to see someone is important, but lots of times, things can be done over the phone, especially with your main medical person. I say it that way because when you are lucky enough to be part of the collaborative practice gang, you get to talk to all the medics at one time or another. And I have been here long enough to have seen the transition from the days when each patient had 'their' doctor and had to wait for that person to be available. It works!

I may have mentioned that I have had my first shot of the Pfizer vaccine. I am scheduled for the second shot in early July. I think I heard that that wait time is being looked at to see if there is enough of the vaccines to allow them to shorten the wait time. I am hoping for an earlier second shot, then I will feel safer, and I will know that I will be protecting others.

With the warmer weather starting, we will be able to have small gatherings (within Dr. Strang's[39] rules) outside. I'm quite sure I am only stat-

---

39   Dr. Robert Strang became Chief Medical Officer of Health for Nova Scotia in 2007.

ing the obvious here, but it feels kind of freeing to say it "out loud".

And now the hammer. When some (very few here, I hope) people de-cide that their rights and freedoms are being taken away because busi-nesses insist on masks, and actually demonstrate against health meas-ures in public, I wonder what on earth they were taught as children about responsibility. There are very, very few people who have breathing problems who can't wear a mask. These folks should stay home and call on the neighbourhood to help them. I think they would find the milk of human kindness would be flowing as people ran around doing everything they could to help.

I was looking at a piece of interesting information about The Black Death back in the 1300s. Apparently, the Renaissance followed after that scourge ravished Europe. Artists and writers and philosophers came for-ward. And after the 1918 Spanish Flu came the Roaring Twenties.

There are various theories about this (aren't there always?) but I would like to think that something similarly good can come of our COVID experience. I think that people are thinking more, I may not agree with them, but thinking is not a bad thing. The inventors are still inventing; the writers are still writing; the poets are still versing; the painters are still painting; the potters are still potting. And any of the other solitary pursuits have probably flourished. We just won't know about it all until the works make their appearance.

I am cheering for all you shut-ins who are creating like mad.

Lightening the load

June 17, 2021

We have now passed the Summer Solstice mark of this 2021st year, *anno domini*. Like many others, I still find it hard to believe we are here. There seems to be a grey, fuzzy, blurry year and months behind us. I hardly re-member what happened during that time.

I do know a couple of things in my head, anyway. I find I am not glued to the television, waiting to see and hear what is going on in the US. After four years of pandemonium and uncertainty and saying OMG every day, it feels very calm. The vestiges are certainly there and I'm not ignoring the news completely but there sure seems to be a sense of relief that a reasonable person is now in charge.

The dreaded virus seems to be letting go of its stranglehold on our days. Mind you, we still have to pay close attention and be really good boys and girls or the wretch may charge back, as it has before. At least at this time of year we are able to get out of our houses, see the plantings that we have been looking at through our windows in the backyard, and possibly even plan for a few gatherings of real, live people.

Remember all those travel plans we had eons ago? Well, I think we can safely start checking our travel points and seeing what our local travel agents have on special for a bit later this year.

Our household has now been fully vaccinated! Two shield wall shots each mean that we can breathe a bit easier and make some plans that stand a chance of being carried out. We are part of the group who were vaccinated against measles, diphtheria, tetanus, pertussis, polio, mumps and rubella. And we get our flu shot every fall.

While the news recently has been pretty awful, world tensions seem to have eased somewhat. I read a daily newsletter from Heather Cox Richardson, who is a historian in Maine. Even her writings, while grimly detailing the continued assault on her country's democracy, have been less dire.

We took a drive around the area last weekend and Annapolis Royal looked like it did umpteen months ago. There were people walking and talking and driving around and going to the market. It was like watching a movie from the olden days! And it felt so normal. And the green every-where is just wonderful to see. I really think the trees have benefited from an easier winter and a wet spring.

In this part of the province, a concerted effort seems to have been made to do our shopping locally. That can mean your local grocery store, pharmacy, farmers' markets, variety stories, restaurants and cafés. These are our neighbours and friends. I'd like to have them around for a long time.

There are, of course, still important issues that we need to deal with these days. Some are more pressing than others, but it feels like things are possible again. And I am very grateful to my fellow Annapolis Valley neighbours for being so careful and caring.

Vaccine passports

August 19, 2021

If having my two Pfizer shots of COVID vaccine and waiting for the requisite two weeks and wearing a mask when with strangers and staying six feet apart makes me safe for and from other human beings—I'll do that gladly.

If getting a Scotia Pass and/or federal vaccine passport means I can let everyone know that I am safe for me and them—I'll do that gladly.

I am fortunate to have travelled all over this country, and in a few other countries, in my lifetime. I distinctly remember that I had to have "all my shots" before going overseas.

My mother was very organized and "all my shots" and some childhood diseases I endured are listed on the back of my birth certificate. The list goes

- Vaccinated (probably Tuberculosis)
- Inoculated against diphtheria
- Inoculated against whooping cough, scarlet fever, tetanus
- Mumps (Contracted)
- Measles (German—Contracted)
- Chicken Pox (Contracted)
- Diphtheria Booster
- Hepatitus A (Contracted)
- Vaccinated (10-year TB booster)
- Salk Vaccine #1 & #2
- Salk Vaccine #3

So, given my Mother's careful work at keeping me safe from the above diseases, why on earth would I trash all that thoughtfulness and not go for the full present-day vaccine program? It would be an insult to her and all those mothers years ago who made sure their kids got the requisite shots. As I recall, some of the shots were given at school—back in the day when there were school nurses.

I may be mistaken, but I believe that, when we moved to Europe, we needed to show proof of vaccinations.

As this pandemic time has moved on and I hear the ridiculous remarks from the so-called "anti-vaxxers", I have gone from "those poor benighted souls with not too much between the ears" to "are you out of your mind!" and on to "stay away from me forever". There are a few other choice words that have erupted, but I'll spare you.

And as I hear the selfish, conniving governors in the US spout their drivel, my thoughts go something like this: as they are mostly Republicans, and as the "anti-vaxxers" are mostly Republicans, we may not have to worry too much longer, as those leaders are killing off their voters.

The clips on TV about those folks who on their deathbeds are saying things like, "I should have got the shot," or, the best one yet, "Can I have the vaccine now?" are pathetic.

Those people who give business owners grief about mask policies: stay home, phone your order in, be polite, don't harass that young person at the checkout behind the Plexiglas shield with their mask on protecting you, who came in to work today to let you do your grocery shopping or get your pills refilled or go to the restaurant.

Of course, there are people who can't have the vaccine for legitimate health reasons. I'm not talking about them.

And if the scientists believe we who have had our two shots, need to get a booster, I'll be signing up as soon as I can. And I will get my flu shot, come the fall.

My body may be a temple, but it is crumbling, and anything I can do to preserve what I can is most welcome.

COVID-19 anniversary

March 9, 2023

On March 16, 2020, I started a Virus Diary blog. Imagine, that was three years ago! I decided to revisit that first entry to see what I said and if I would change anything, knowing what I know now.

Here is what I wrote:

Monday, March 16, 2020

After listening to our Prime Minister yesterday (Sunday), I decided that I would stay at home starting today.

This is not a complete hardship for me these days. I am 79 and, therefore, in a high-risk group. I have, as they say, pre-existing heart issues. All is under control with meds, so I am fine. The last appointment with the cardiac guy was re-assuring—he said my heart was good even after a stent a number of years ago and a recent atrial fibrillation diagnosis. My mobility is rather ghastly —legs don't work as well as they should.

You should know that every conversation with an "older" person either starts or ends with the Health Report! And then somewhere in there is the Weather Report! ☺

I am worried about my relatives and friends who go to the warmer climes in the winter. My sister, my sister-in-law and my good friend all are or were in Florida this winter. My friend is now across the border, and I will be talking to her soon once she's home here. Now that I am self-isolating, I won't actually see her for a while (who knows how long this will last?).

My sister-in-law is due to fly home on Thursday—thank goodness! Flights are being cancelled and borders are being more stringent. I have not heard when my sister is coming home but I hope it's soon. I saw this morning that some insurance companies won't cover anything out-of-country after March 23. What a lousy bunch! Stronger language comes to mind!

I am retired. I do volunteer work these days. I can do computer work from home. I can catch up on The Family Tree. I can write countless emails and annoy every relative and friend I have —be prepared! I can post stuff on Facebook. I can continue to re-file correspondence and jpgs. I can cull ephotos. I can watch TV. I can watch movies on Netflix. There are green things coming up in the garden which I may have to shuffle outside to see. And I can call my excellent friends to see how they are doing.

Speaking of friends, I had four calls in less than 24 hours from dear souls who wanted to know if they could pick up anything or do anything for me. I love them all! And I know that "love" is a word that gets thrown around a lot these days but this time, I really mean it!

Onward.

And now we are three years away. I have had every shot they are willing to give me. I still have a mask in my jacket pocket, just in case. I still don't go out much.

However, I am still sending emails, having phone calls, posting stuff on Facebook and, so far, have not been attacked by the virus.

Onward, indeed!

Friends and Neighbours

I have friends all over the place. Certainly here in Canada but also in the US, Australia, France and Luxembourg. I have had lots of neighbours over the years as well. That's what happens when you have lived in nine provinces and two territories and in Luxembourg. Friends have been bosom buddies and the kin you meet every once in a while, and feel comfortable taking up where you left off.

As I get older, I have lost some friends and certainly relatives. It seems odd to say that I am now the matriarch of my family – the oldest of my generation. All the generation before me have gone. Here are some columns about friends and neighbours.

Anne Crossman's

Neighbours

January 14, 2021

While the word "neighbours" implies "right next door", I have neighbours both near and far. I have stretched the word to include those people who have helped me over the years, or are still helping but from a bit further away.

I live in rural Nova Scotia. My next-door neighbours include a farming family on one side with a librarian in the household. A horse farmer has the property on the other side and across the highway. And there's a garage just down the way. There's a retired handyman just over the road. There's an Annapolis County employee up the road and there's a nurse and her husband, who is presently doing security work around the county, along with a librarian son who works at COGS (Centre for Geographic Sciences, part of the Nova Scotia Community College).

And there are some new people I haven't met yet. The lady who cuts my hair and works with international students is up the road. Then comes the man who does just about everything—painting, gyprocking, etc., etc. And his wife helps when she's not working at a hardware store. And the new people (they've only been here a year or so) from British Columbia who are retired university folks, and she can sing like mad. And the previous warden (who also makes harps and can play them really well) and his lovely family live close to my little community.

In the middle of it all are the Centrelea Community Hall, built in 1867 and the United Baptist Church, built in 1853. Some of the families have been here for quite a few generations, some are sort of new, and some are really new.

This is what my neighbours have done over these past 22 years:

- Brought me a lovely basket of goodies when I was laid up in my hospital bed in the dining room, after a hip replacement.
- Put yeast and eggs and cottage cheese in my mailbox with a money exchange to help me when I went into COVID-19 bread-

baking mode. That's over now, by the way.

- Looked after Sally (the dog) when there was one of those emergency things. Sally loves that neighbour now.
- When we decided to have a COVID-19 Canada Day party in the backyard under three awnings for social distancing, folks turned up with an amazing bunch of food.
- When a lovely neighbour decided we should have a carol-sing evening at our Hall, it turned out to be wonderful, with kids singing and a pianist and a harpist and song sheets. That was a very special time.
- All the great potluck dinners we had with the most amazing food and great company on birthdays, Christmases and New Year's Eves.
- And the parties with oodles of folks who came after tourist season was done and we could exchange silly (and sometimes fabulous) gifts.
- Then there was the time three of us (all from this neighbourhood) decided we should celebrate the 100th birthday of Ernest Buckler (author of *The Mountain and the Valley*) and we did, even though we really didn't know what we were doing. It was great.
- All the great lunches and dinners and potluck Christmases we had at the Hall.

The people change over time. New people move in, some pass away, some move away, but the neighbourhood continues to operate. It isn't the way it was 75 years ago, but it has found its new way, with new ideas and new people.

And COVID-19 won't change that.

Tragedy and grief

January 28, 2021

When the scallop boat *Chief William Saulis* went down before Christmas, it was a reminder that the fates have not finished with us yet in Nova

Scotia. The vessel itself was recently found on the bottom of the Bay of Fundy, off Delaps Cove.

With the COVID-19 plague hanging over us since early last year, the Portapique massacre, the loss of two Nova Scotian Armed Forces personnel in separate accidents, and the six who went down in the Bay, 28 people died, seemingly unnecessarily, in 2020. The April 29 crash of a Canadian Forces helicopter in the Mediterranean Sea claimed the lives of six military members—all of them based in the Halifax area. Then, on May 6, the province learned of the disappearance of a three-year-old boy from Truro who had been walking near a brook with his grandmother.

And there were the personal losses of close friends and the worry about relatives and friends with severe illnesses. This time of year reminds us of parents who have gone, and favourite relatives who left too soon.

There are no pat answers for all this. There are books, and there are those wonderful grief counsellors who try to help out. Everyone has to find their own best way to cope with the sadness and the worry and the grief.

I have tried to avoid going on and on about the COVID virus. I think each of us just has to find our best way to deal with it. I hardly go anywhere. I am fortunate to have a built-in shopper who goes regularly to the grocery store, the pharmacy and, occasionally, to the Annapolis Royal Farmers Market. He does all this with his mask on (we both got lovely new ones for Christmas) and keeps his distance.

I went to a Chamber of Commerce meeting in December with five other people who were seated so far apart we had to yell at each other to be heard.

Christmas in Bridgetown was just great, by the way, with the house decorating contest and the tree decorating by the old Town Hall by the youngsters from the school; and there were Christmas trees decorated with various themes on street corners. I had to do a bit of a drive around to see that.

And did you see that wonderful steam engine getting transported from Upper Clements Park to the Middleton train station? The photos and videos were terrific. What a great idea! Thanks to all who made it happen.

As you can see, I have drifted away from the theme this week. For me, veering off the topic of tragedy and grief is my way of coping. Give the latest piece of bad news its due, worry it around a bit, take a deep breath and move on to something else. Revisit it every now and then for as much as you can take, and then move on again.

There are folks who grieve publicly and those who grieve quietly to themselves. Sometimes it works and sometimes it doesn't.

And then someone has a baby. And the grandmas go bananas. I know a few like that. So hope and newness arrive and make us smile again. And we can just tuck the grief in a pocket or a purse, to bring out when the house is quiet and the fire is dying and it's time to go to bed.

January and February are long months, and this year they will especially be lengthy with this virus. We will get through this dark time. I'm pretty sure.

Volunteers

February 18, 2021

Every year around this time the call goes out from your municipal government to send in the name of a volunteer who has made a difference in their community for whatever reason. Over the years many have been named and have been asked to a presentation ceremony, and have been applauded for their good deeds.

I haven't found out how long this celebration of the volunteer has been going on, but I think I remember that it's been around at least 15 or 20 years, possibly even longer.

Since most of the volunteers, with few exceptions, have been people in their "later" years, there has been an endless supply. But will that continue?

The various organizations I have belonged to in these parts for 22 years still have people doing the work. But there seems to be fewer than there used to be. The skills required to be a volunteer have changed as well. It used to be that cooking and baking skills were a must. That's how the community halls managed to survive. And if there was a handy guy in the community, he would help with the painting or the roofing as long as the hall would buy the paint or the shingles. And there would be a day set aside when the place just buzzed with laughter, sandwiches and tea, and the work would get done with volunteers.

Food became the mainstay for raising funds to keep the lights on and the furnace running, and to make the repairs required to some of these old buildings. There were takeout lunches for Mother's and Father's Day. There were potluck gatherings for the family and friends of those who passed away. There were birthday parties for kids. And there were sit-down lunches and dinners in the fall. And, of course, there was the Christmas potluck dinner, with a visit from Santa Claus.

While the past eleven months have been hard on all kinds of local businesses, they have also been hard on the volunteer community. Wracking their brains for fund-raising ideas and fun community things to do has been difficult.

Community halls aren't the only volunteer-dependent organizations. There are your local museums, which are under great stress for a number of reasons. The volunteer fire departments are always in need—witness their 50/50 raffles going on Facebook these days. Churches are not as full as they used to be. Chambers of Commerce, and Boards of Trade, in small communities are getting smaller.

The calls continue to go out for people to serve on provincial advisory boards and many regional boards of directors. It's becoming harder to ask people to give up time, money and brain power to sit on some of these boards. Many provincial boards have been reduced to "advisory" roles. And that's exactly what it means—advice only. And of course, there is no compensation other than travel costs for some meetings.

In this Time of COVID, grant writing has become a skill many organizations rely on to bring in money. As we go forward, I would like to encourage any group looking for money from their fellow taxpayers to add in the number of hours that volunteers put in the run of a year—board meetings, emails, paying bills, cleaning, checking on the facility, cooking and baking—and list those hours in the spot on the form for in-kind contributions. As of April 1, 2021 the minimum wage is $12.95 per hour. While this may not do anything to persuade the funders, it will indicate the value that those volunteers put in to do something good and worthwhile for their community.

Take a look around your community. Look at what would *not* be there if it weren't for volunteers—community halls, churches, lighthouses, fire departments, museums, artists' co-operatives, drama groups, choirs, community bands, beautification groups, heritage protection organizations, town and county advisory committees, Lions Clubs, Legions, sports organizations, and on and on.

If you have some free time, think about giving some of it to support the organizations and good causes in the place where you reside. Be one of those people who can be counted on. Don't be shy: those volunteers are usually a good bunch to hang out with and they almost always can bake a cake at the drop of a hat.

Travelling in Canada's North

March 25, 2021

Every now and then, a quiz pops up online that asks where you have been and where you have lived. This kind of quiz is usually devised by someone in the backrooms of a data miner to let them know the likes and dislikes of possible marketing targets. It's kind of a shame, because the quizzes are fun to do, and they also give a peek into what friends have done in their lives.

Most of my travels have been in Canada. Possibly the most memorable part of the country for me has been the North.

It's funny how things from one's childhood influence where you go and what you do as you grow older. As far as I can determine, two things led me North: Jack London's book *The Call of the Wild* and a young girl-friend's older sister, who worked for the federal Department of Indian and Northern Development (as it was known then. It was dissolved in 2019 and the Department of Indigenous Services Canada and the Department of Crown-Indigenous Relations and Northern Affairs Canada took over its responsibilities).

It turns out that Jack London was kind of a radical guy. I didn't know that at the time, but it was interesting to find out that he hung out with other writer and artists, and lived quite the Bohemian lifestyle[40].

Getting back to his book, the story of the Yukon and the dog and the countryside and the adventure got to me as it did to many. Please don't watch the latest movie version—it's quite dreadful.

My girlfriend's older sister, Maureen, would sit in the kitchen and tell stories of the possibility of going North with her job. There were clerical

---

40   britannica.com/biography/Jack-London

and secretarial jobs in Northern communities. She talked about meeting Northern people who came South occasionally, and she found them "very interesting."

All the above must have stuck with me. After I married, a time came when a job interview took our family to Yellowknife. On November 11, 1977. With two young people. With two dogs. With 13 pieces of baggage. In a snowstorm. The one cat arrived the next day.

All kinds of people from the CBC station came to pick us up and take us to the Yellowknife Inn, where we stayed until our housing was ready. That was the start of a big, important part of my life and my education.

One of the highlights of my time in the North was being in Sachs Harbour for the signing of the Agreement in Principle for the Inuvialuit Final Agreement on October 31, 1978. Sachs Harbour is on Banks Island, north of the Mackenzie River Delta that flows into the Beaufort Sea. I was working for *NEWS of the NORTH* then, a weekly paper in Yellowknife. Eric Watt, a PR guy with the territorial government, called me early one morning. "Pack a toothbrush, the plane is leaving before noon for Sachs."

It was quite an exciting time.

A few years later, I was fortunate to be promoted to Operations Manager at the CBC Northern Service's radio station in Rankin Inlet, on the west coast of Hudson's Bay. I worked for one of the most interesting people I have ever met. Jose Kusugak was funny, generous, intelligent, inquisitive and a leading light in the younger Inuit leadership.

I gave myself a stern talking-to when I went there: keep your eyes and ears open and your mouth shut. I learned a lot about how the Inuit lived, and their customs and generosity. And I came away saying this about Rankin Inlet: the weather was atrocious, and the people were wonderful.

I will tell more tales from the North as time goes on. In the meantime, stay safe, be kind and get your COVID-19 vaccination as soon as you can.

Take time to celebrate

September 1, 2022

It struck me recently that I have longtime friends who are very sick, and I have some longtime friends who have found a love after a long time. And although those two thoughts don't seem connected, they are, in that I realize that I am fortunate to have many friends all over the place. I keep in touch.

I have known one person for nearly 40 years, a work colleague, for sure, but a good friend over time. Another person I have known for about the same time, once again a work colleague who became a good friend. I have another longtime friend who has been sick for quite a few years. She has a wicked sense of humour and sends me deep-thinking emails along with positively hilarious stuff.

All of these fine people have very serious illnesses and have shared their experiences. This is kind of remarkable to me. They have shared their stories with grace along the way.

It always does my heart good to hear a love story. One friend seems to have found a mate late in life and is very happy by all accounts. He has had a rough time over the years, and I am so pleased that he is happy. The same thing has happened to at least two other friends: they found a lover and a friend later in life and they all seem to be very happy.

In thinking about aging and lives lived, I went to a 90th birthday party for a neighbour here in my community. It was held at our local community hall. I haven't seen the hall so filled with happy, smiling people for a very long time. So a birthday party can bring the neighbours out. And the cake was excellent. The doors were open and there was lots of air circulation. Some folks wore masks.

While people in this province seem to have forgotten that we were the best in the country with the COVID-19 business for about two years. We were the envy of not only other parts of this country but of other countries as well. We have fallen off the "be very, very careful" wagon. Seeing friends outside in the summer seems to be all right but I am seeing more and more people not taking the precautions we once heard Dr. Strang tell us to take. That message seems to be much more muted these days from the good doctor.

And now to stitch all these thoughts together—friendships, love in later life, gatherings for special occasions and the pandemic. I won't go into a whole ramble about the reason for living—I'd just get a bit maudlin. But I have all these life experiences moving around in my mind and it seems to me we need to take the time to celebrate the good bits because, before you know it, there won't be time for any more good bits.

Our people

October 28, 2021

According to the latest figure I could find, there are well over 20,000 residents of Annapolis County. While I have lived in many places around Canada, this is where I have lived the longest—over 21 years now. These years have given me a chance to meet such a wide variety of people. These people have coloured my life and enriched it with their talents and skills and caring. Twenty thousand people is rather a small bunch in the grand scheme of things, especially when compared to other municipal units in this world.

We have poets, writers, playwrights, story tellers, song writers, painters of all kinds, musicians, fishers, chefs, sommeliers, sculptors, singers, costumiers, dancers of various kinds and ages, doctors, nurses, nurse practitioners, map makers, photographers, potters, videographers, firemen/women, web designers, gardeners, historians, mycologists, biologists, brew masters, lawyers, shoemakers, hair dressers, pedicurists, genealogists, coffee roasters, bakers, publishers, grocers, carpenters, masons, drywallers, pharmacists, printers, picture framers, actors, farmers, store owners, knitters, pilots, cement makers, road builders, vintners, vehicle fixers and dealers, soccer players, cricketers, oodles of different crafts people, and probably far more skilled people whom I have missed.

And that is within Annapolis County alone. It struck me that, if you live here, you might not have to travel very far to live well here. We can buy almost everything a person would need right here. We have many volunteers doing amazing work for this community.

I would really like us to celebrate what we have and whom we have as neighbours. I do. I appreciate every one of the people in the many categories above. I have run into many of them. I know many of them. Many of them are friends. They work hard at their vocation/profession. They take care of us. They entertain us. They teach us their skills gladly. They feed us. They brighten our homes. They write about us and take photographs of us and fly drones above us to show us where we live in a whole new way.

While I expect many rural communities in Canada can say the same, I wonder how many of us pay attention to these truths. It's possible that the Time of COVID has brought these feelings to the fore. If so, I am grateful. There is a lot of other bumpf and stuff and idiocy and meanness around these days that is out in the open. I would like to use the really good bits to face down those bad bits.

With respect, here endeth the lesson.

PS – Did anyone find it rather odd (to say the least) to get a flyer in your mailbox from Canada Post about a "MyMoney Loan"? My read says this federal Crown Corporation has teamed up with TD Bank to just offer loans, in response to pressure to provide the sort of full-service postal banking we had 50 years ago. What the heck is going on here?

Health – Mine and Others'

There are now more conversations with folks that start off with, "How are you?" or even, "How *are* you?" After four or more paragraphs during which various health issues are discussed, comes the, "How is so-and-so?" This refers to relatives, usually, even though we sometimes get to friends' health issues as well.

Cancer

December 15, 2022

I will be getting an early Christmas present tomorrow: a medical proced-ure (that's what we used to call an "operation").

I have breast cancer. These are words that were hardly ever said out loud until relatively recently. And strangely, it wasn't usually because the word "cancer" was taboo, although it was said in whispers. It was that, in our puritanical culture, the word "breast" was hardly mentioned out loud because it had to do with sex.

Everyone deals with this kind of diagnosis in their own way, I really understand that. I am hoping that telling my version of this disease will help someone else, should it happen to them.

Some of my ancestors had breast cancer. My paternal grandmother died with it, as did one of my paternal aunts. My other paternal aunt had a lumpectomy. My sister has had a lumpectomy. I have had skin cancer, a basal cell carcinoma on my face.

There do not seem to be any people (that I know of) on my mother's side of the family, but then it wasn't talked about very much back in the day.

So I would seem to be fortunate in that I found the lump relatively early and will be getting my Christmas present lumpectomy tomorrow at the Valley Regional Hospital. And it all has happened quickly.

I say all this because I now know a few friends who have had breast cancer. And more are letting me know about theirs. It seems that the dam has broken, and women are able to share this important information.

I am very grateful to all of them for telling me that they are getting on with their lives. They are getting on without one breast or they are get-ting on with a breast scarred from the lumpectomy operation.

Telling people about it has helped me, partly because that's how I deal with issues. Talking about some problems with relatives and close friends has always been helpful for me. I know that some people might squirm a bit, so I don't say anything to them. I don't want to make them uncomfortable.

I am fortunate to have a good family doctor and now a good surgeon, by all accounts. The office people in both these practices are great, too.

They must hear some hard stories, both in their offices and over the phone.

Apparently, my operation will be day surgery. That may mean I'll be home tomorrow evening—we'll see.

I promise to be a lot cheerier in time for the Ho! Ho! Ho! Time.

Neighbours

January 19, 2023

I am gradually getting to meet our new neighbours here in Annapolis Royal. I want to start by saying that I am talking about those people who live next door, or one door over.

I have had many neighbours over the years. Some were people who lived next door, but many were folks who have had like interests or have become neighbours by virtue of that great phrase "we just hit it off right away".

Some I have stayed in touch with over the years as I have moved across the country. I tend to think of them as more than acquaintances or work colleagues or best friends—they have become part of my neighbourhood of the mind and heart.

The net is wide, from all sides of this country to across the "pond" in Europe and even as far away as Oz. The variety is rather astounding when I stop to think about them all.

There is a retired wine columnist/pharmacist; quite a few retired Indigenous broadcasters; a ranching family in Alberta; a highly-regarded retired businessman in Europe; a girlfriend from my teens now in the US; a couple of inn-keeping couples; a bunch of retired broadcasters across this country; a retired radical newspaper editor; a couple of mayors and a few municipal councillors; and dear friends in Belgium. Of course, there are others, but the list was getting a tad long.

These "neighbours" now include the Annapolis Royal folks who will, I feel, move into their new slot in my mind as friends with whom to plan block parties once the weather warms up.

I moved to this neighbourhood from a neighbourhood. There were people who lived just down the road and with whom I worked to keep the community vibrant. I keep those people in my neighbourhood file as well. It was 24 years of living together—a bit spread out, in the rural way —but still living together.

Of course, I have very close friends who know most of my secrets and put up with my silly jokes or my occasional emotional outburst. They go under the heading of Very Special Neighbours.

If my musing about neighbours has rung a little bell, you might like to run through the list of all the folks in your own neighbourhood. You might be pleasantly surprised.

PS - As I talked about a couple of weeks ago[41], I was scheduled for a lumpectomy to remove a probable small cancer in my right breast. I thought I'd bring you up to date this week.

The procedure happened on Friday, January 6 at the Valley Regional Hospital in Kentville. After some pre-operation work the day before and a night at Fidelis House, I arrived at the hospital at 7:30 in the morning.

After various and sundry things happened throughout the day, I was out of the building at 5 in the afternoon and driven home by 6.

It went like clockwork. I didn't wait for more than maybe 20 minutes between those "sundry" things. The people were wonderful, friendly, and caring, checking up on me at every turn.

I do have to wait a while to see what happens next, but, other than some bruising which will go away soon, I am relieved to have this go so smoothly. I should hear soon what was found and I'll let you know.

I want to thank everyone at the hospital and medical office there for the care.

---

41   See the previous column.

Fundy Hospice Gala

May 4, 2023

The first annual Fundy Hospice Gala was held last Saturday at The Digby Pines Resort and Spa. It was quite the "do", as my Grandma used to say.

While I sort of knew what a hospice is, I thought I'd have a look to see what I could find. The word comes from Latin "hospitum", meaning a place of rest and protection for the sick and tired. It is believed that the first ones were in Malta, caring for the pilgrims going to and from the Holy Land. In the early 1300s, the order of the Knights Hospitaller of St. John of Jerusalem opened the first hospice in Rhodes.

Hospice care these days applies to places where people can be looked after at the end of their lives. They are made comfortable by reducing pain and suffering according to the patient's and/or the family's wishes.

The Atalanta Hospice Society's mission is to offer respectful, dignified and caring support for end-of-life care. This is the group raising the $5.5 million to build the Fundy Hospice. I saw the plans for the hospice, to be built in Cornwallis Park on the residential side of the highway. It was designed by Harry Jost, Annapolis Royal Architect, in consultation with the board of directors.

By the way, the society took the name Atalanta from the 17-cannon ship commanded by Admiral Robert Digby, who helped evacuate about 1,500 United Empire Loyalists from the United States arriving in Conway (renamed Digby in 1787) in early June of 1783, at the end of the American War of Independence.

I have lived long enough to have had relatives and friends die. I have seen and known of friends who should have been in a pleasant, airy, comfortable room of their own where family and friends could visit, with an armchair in which the person could could sit and look out a window. They weren't. And it wasn't because the family didn't want it, or the medical profession didn't want it. It was because there just wasn't that kind of facility close enough to get to easily or quickly.

I was able to find ten hospices in Nova Scotia. The closest to Annapolis and Digby Counties (including Annapolis Royal, Middleton, and Digby) are one on the South Shore, in Bridgewater. There is one in Wolfville and another in Kentville. They are a bit far to be visiting a relative who is dying and may only have a few weeks to live.

Having seen the plans for the new hospice in Cornwallis Park, I was happy to contribute to the fundraiser last weekend. The dinner was good. The company at our table was interesting. And we saw some folks we haven't seen in some time. Folks were having a great time with the auctioneering. The most fun was hearing the bidding for the incomparable Linda Bailey's (Priceless) Coconut Cream Pie, which went for $400.

Should the occasion arise in the future, knowing the generosity of the community which contributed to the building of this peaceful and beautiful place, I would be pleased to spend my remaining days here.

Managing the medications

May 18, 2023

I have a weekly routine which occasionally gets a bit off schedule, which, in turn, leads me to be putting my pills in those little seven-day pill holders before I have my coffee in the morning.

It seems to me that as we age, the more pills we take, just for our general welfare and keeping us alive. And more or less with it.

I was wondering the other morning, as I had all the bottles out on the dining room table—they require that much space now—how had it reached this point?

I take five prescription pills in the morning, sometimes seven—it depends on how things are going. I take two non-prescription ones as well. And then I take three more just in case. You have to take some of these with food, you understand, but for others it doesn't matter, but it's best to get them in early.

And then there's lunchtime. I take one prescription pill and four non-prescription ones. I want you to understand that all these pills are ones the doctor told me to take. Why would I take anything they didn't recommend?

Just this past week, I had another one added to suppertime. I have to take that one with food, too.

And now we move into the evening. There are two prescription ones with water and an hour later there is one prescription pill and two non-prescription ones.

And that's it.

I am very fond of the all the folks at Bridgetown Pharmasave and have been going to see them every now and then when my resident guy is busy doing more important things. I call up, give them the number on the little bottle, and it's ready and waiting.

There are a few things I've noticed as I've gotten older. The most important thing is: **don't drop the pill!** The wretched things blend into the carpet. Then you have to bend over in a most awkward way—no description necessary—and try to pick the little suckers up! When we had a dog, I lived in great fear that she would think that it was sort of like popcorn: if it fell on the floor, it belonged to her. Heaven knows what some of those meds would do to a dog!

And then comes the day when the usual collection of pills for that particular time of day is missing one. I have two little egg cups that I use to keep everything straight. The loss of that little sort-of beige pill that I take at lunch time can cause great consternation. Did I mistakenly take it at breakfast? Did I miss putting it in last night or yesterday morning—you know, that morning before coffee?

I have to go back to the beginning—all the while mumbling to myself and saying things like, "Where the hell would it have gone?" and, "Do you suppose I took two by mistake?"

The resident guy ignores these mumblings, which is a good thing because who knows what I might say next.

In spite of all that, pills are a very good thing in my case. They are keeping me going and I am grateful!

Call 988

December 7, 2023

"Good Afternoon, The 4th ESTATE."

There was a long pause. And then a woman's tired voice said, "Is this the Help Line?"

"Yes, you have reached The 4th ESTATE's weekly newspaper, and we have a Help Line."

"I need help. Can you help me?"

"Maybe. Can you tell me what the problem seems to be? I hope I can help."

And so began one of the longest, most important phone calls I have ever had in my working life. This took place in the early 1970s.

This woman sounded so low. Very quietly, she said she had nothing more to live for.

I was very concerned and started to talk calmly, asking a couple of easy questions. "What can you see out your window today?" "Do you have anyone to talk to?" "Do you live in town?"

And then I just babbled with things like, "If you leave now, you will miss the leaves turning in fall. You wouldn't want to miss that."

We were on the phone for a long time, I don't know how long. I was exhausted at the end. I believe I gave her a phone number to call with someone who had real qualifications to help her.

I remember every part of that conversation with a sad lady over 50 years ago in Halifax.

A month or so later: "Good morning, The 4th ESTATE."

A long pause.

"That's the voice I remember!" a smiling voice came back.

This nice lady went on to say she had called the number I had given her, but she wanted to thank me so much for listening and talking to her.

It was one of the scariest, most satisfying, most moving events in my life to know that I had helped someone. It was scary because I was not qualified to give this lady advice. It was satisfying because she got help. It was moving because a stranger needed an ear and a gentle, caring voice.

I can't remember where she called after talking to me. But if you ever get a call from a friend or acquaintance, you can now tell them to call 988.[42]

This story still gives me goosebumps and makes me reach for the tissues.

---

42 In 2024, Moose House published *The Non-Therapist*, designed to help people who find themselves in a situation like this, where they need to offer help beyond their expertise: moosehousepress.com/product-page/the-non-therapist

Anne Crossman's

News of the World

Having done a lot of research on my parents' lives during World War II, and having lived in the Grand Duchy of Luxembourg in my teenage years, I have always been interested in what goes on beyond my own country. Like most people, war is horrific to me. I have seen the aftermath. And we are all given a daily blast of war on our TV screens.

My parents and my grandparents were Royalists to the core. Given that my parents were Elizabeth and Philip and I am Anne, we are not too far removed from that royal family, I like to think.

Anne Crossman's

Journalism

October 14, 2021

> The Norwegian Nobel Committee has decided to award the Nobel Peace Prize for 2021 to Maria Ressa and Dmitry Muratov for their efforts to safeguard freedom of expression, which is a pre-condition for democracy and lasting peace. – news release

When the above announcement was made last week, I sent out a cheer and a wish. The two journalists who were honoured are amongst the many brave and principled people on this planet. The cheer is for the important work that they do, and the wish is that they stay safe.

I have been in the media business off and on since 1969, in Halifax. While I haven't been a reporter during all that time, I have seen the good, bad and the ugly that happens in this business.

I watched really good people sweat blood (and sometimes tears) over a story, making sure all the facts were correct, checking with people they would really not like to speak with, agonizing over the consequences of the story, being angry that nothing was being done to rectify a situation, drinking a bit too much after a long day, and cheering when that story made a difference for some person who was being kicked around.

Dealing with the human experiences of grief, anger, rage, suffering, starvation, and injustice takes a huge toll on reporters.

I see CBC's Susan Ormiston is in Afghanistan. I see Brian Stewart is in Russia. I fear for their safety. There are many who died because they told the dangerous story. Dimitry Muratov dedicated his Nobel prize to six journalists who were killed in Russia because they were doing their jobs.

And there were those reporters who told the real story of what was going on in the Vietnam War. They didn't toe the line that the military and the government had established to feed pure propaganda/lies to the folks back home.

Today's Canadian media people are being attacked for doing their jobs. We are not immune to this hateful practice. I recommend an interview CBC Radio's Day 6 did with Supriya Dwivedi, senior counsel for the public relations firm Enterprise Canada and a former radio host for Global News. She tells a horrific story of abuse and fear.

While a statement was released by many media outlets about how shocked and appalled they were about the treatment of their reporters, there didn't seem to be much in the statement about how they were going to protect their employees.

And so all the people in the reporting business whom I have met and admired over the years are, in a way, part of this Nobel Peace Prize.

What might surprise you is that they really care. And they want to get the story right. And they really don't get paid anything close to what they are worth.

Ukraine again

March 24, 2022

> We have no real concept of the ravages of war. We can sit and watch the news and think how awful it is—just imagine having to toss a few bits into a back pack and leave your home, your town, your country. We are all citizens of the world, and we must unite to support one another against the evils of war.
>
> – Elizabeth McMichael

As the news channels continue to show the heartbreak and devastation in Ukraine and its president continues to remind western governments that his country is fighting for its life, I hope that the ways and means can be found in a timely, nay, speedy fashion to get some of those people here to ride out the terror until they can go home again to rebuild what the tyrant has destroyed.

I got to thinking about the Pearson Peacekeeping Centre (1994-2013) that was headquartered in Cornwallis Park. Annapolis County Councillor for District 6 Alex Morrison spoke about the Centre and the connections around the world in some of the 'hard places' at last week's County Council meeting.

Of course, there are all kinds of stories about why it closed, and I won't go into that here. I was always a big fan of Canada's blue-bereted Peacekeepers, too.

I sure like the idea of being just down the road from the Annapolis Basin Conference Centre in Cornwallis Park, which may be doing its bit to help refugees feel safe.

History is a funny thing. It depends on who is writing it and who is re-membering it. I know people who remember World War II very well. It was awful for them. They were liberated by Russians.

My aunt and uncle went to Russia in 1961 with a British tour group— by boat from London to St. Petersburg, then by bus to Moscow and across Belarus, Poland *et al*, and back to London.

While they were in Berlin, "The Wall"[43] started to go up.

Which brings us to the Cold War. I know about that. I remember the Airlift to and from Berlin getting goods in and out. It started on June 24, 1948 and lasted almost a year. The Soviets blockaded rail, road, and water access to Allied-controlled areas of Berlin. My father was in the RCAF, and he was posted to a NATO base in Germany in 1953, along with other countries' officers.

So I have been on the fringes of war, but I have never, I am thankful, been in a war. I have seen the aftermath—the rebuilding of homes and buildings from the stone rubble in the tiny country of Luxembourg after 1945. I have heard the stories, read the books, seen the movies, and never want to have anything to do with war—ever.

Yet here we are, watching yet another war. It is disheartening and tragic to see this one added to a long list of human suffering.

Here are some of the wars since 1945:

India-Pakistan	Cyprus	Ireland	Afghanistan
Israel-Palestine	Vietnam	Falklands	Iraq
Malaya	Suez	Gulf War	Libya
Korea	Brunei	Sierra Leone	Syria
Cuba	Indonesia	Bosnia	Yemen
Kenya	Aden	Kosovo	

---

43   The Berlin Wall, dividing the city and, by extension, East and West Germany, went up in 1961 to prevent people fleeing from the east to the west. It started to come down in 1989. en.wikipedia.org/wiki/Berlin_Wall

And there are more. It's worth looking them up.
    It is daunting.
    "Where Have All the Flowers Gone?"

Royal-watching

June 9, 2022

I was up very early last week to watch some of the first day of Queen Elizabeth II's Platinum Jubilee celebrations. Like many here in Canada, I have watched the Queen throughout the years as she dealt with all the regal duties and the family fiascos and triumphs.

My first memory is when Elizabeth was still a princess and newly married to Philip. In 1951, they arrived in Ottawa on the train and, after various visits around the capital, they drove around Lansdowne Park in an open car. I was in the grandstand. It was quite exciting.

I made a scrapbook of all kinds of newspaper clippings, and there were some special editions with just pictures. I have no idea what happened to that bulging book with bits of glue and folded pages holding those treasures.

The next time I saw her was when she was Queen. She and Prince Philip arrived at the Air Force Base in St. Hubert, Quebec in June 1959. My father had been posted there (RCAF Air Defence Command Headquarters) and we lived in the PMQs (Personnel Married Quarters).

There was a big tent set up out on the tarmac to receive the Queen and her party. It was a sizzling hot day. We were able to watch all this, in-cluding Prince Philip opening up the back of the tent to let some air in. She was probably feeling pretty queasy, both with the heat and the fact that she was pregnant with Prince Andrew.

After the reception on the base, my parents and I went to Montreal to watch the official opening of the St. Lawrence Seaway. There was Queen Elizabeth, the Duke of Edinburgh, and President Dwight D. Eisenhower giving speeches and waving to the crowds. And Prime Minister John Diefenbaker was there representing Canada. The yacht *Britannia* sailed through the St. Lambert lock and the Seaway was officially opened.

And so, I have sort of paid attention over the years to what the Queen and her family were doing. I don't think it was an obsession, but I did find it interesting. My perspective changed as I grew older and paid more attention to the politics of having a monarch be the head of state of one's country.

The fact that she was never meant to be queen but suddenly, at age 10 or so, realizing that was going to be her fate must have been a bit hard to deal with. The abdication of her uncle gave her father a job that he really didn't want. But he did his best, as they say.

There were the deaths and the divorces and the other grievous goings-on that must have made her pretty angry and sad. But she carried on.

It has been sobering to see her, such a tiny little figure still in a hat and hanging on to Philip's walking staff and trying to celebrate 70 years doing her job. Many people retire at 65, and look at her: 31 years past that age and still doing her job as best she can.

I probably should tell you that my mother's name was Elizabeth (never Betty or Beth) and my father's name was Philip and my name is Anne. That makes it kind of mandatory to be a royal watcher, don't you think?

The Royals

September 22, 2022

I may have mentioned in a previous column that my mother's name was Elizabeth and my father's name was Philip. While we did not have a Charles in the family, we certainly had an Anne: me.

As we seem to be remembering where we were when we saw the Queen, I thought I'd talk about my recollections this week.

First, let me say that a fine person has died. Elizabeth II had a good innings—96 is pretty good. It seemed like her mind held but her poor, frail physical parts were going fast. Imagine hanging on long enough to welcome the new Prime Minister with the "kissing the hands" ceremony.

Like many around the world, I was an admirer of the woman. I am rather ambivalent about the whole monarchy business, but not so about Queen Elizabeth. She did her duty to the end. She was interested in the people and the places of the world, wherever she went.

She treated people with respect. She was rarely critical. And she had a wonderful twinkle in her eye on occasion, which meant lots to those who heard her small, funny remarks.

I have been watching all the television coverage over the past two weeks of the Queen's death and legacy, and the transition to the new King. I am fortunate that I am able to do this. It reminded me of watching other world events on television over the years. I was glued to the TV after John F. Kennedy was shot in 1963. I saw Lee Harvey Oswald, who shot Kennedy, get shot himself on live TV while I was watching over my first wee daughter in her crib in the living room as she suffered from chickenpox. I stayed with that TV for three days.

A friend reminded me that before television was in every home, there were the Pathé newsreels one saw at the movies before the feature. For me, that was Saturday afternoons.

And so, there is a before and after part of my thoughts these days. Before, it might take days, even weeks for momentous news to reach everyone. The newspapers during World War II carried stories filed by telegraph from overseas for Canadians. Radio was a bit faster and more immediate.

But television has brought the world into our homes and lives like nothing else. Seeing those videos and clips and live shots by drone is quite remarkable when you think about it.

It's too bad people are in a very bad mood these days. Imagine complaining about having a national holiday to commemorate the work and the personage of Queen Elizabeth II. It's one day out of your very important life, folks. Take a deep breath.

Things will be different with King Charles III. He is a different person. Things change over time. Attitudes change over time. People change, too.

Flying the Ukrainian flag

March 2, 2023

As I went back over my column to edit and pull it together this week, an old memory from Echternach in Luxembourg floated to the top. I was standing in the pretty park at the bend in a river, looking at the Pavilion built in 1765.

I was shocked when I first had a glimpse of what happened to that lovely structure in the little town just across the Sauer, or Sûre, River from Germany in 1953. There is a photo taken in 1945 after World War II, when war charged through the town. And there is a photo taken in 2013 when I saw it again. The Siegfried Line had a bunker just across that river. I know, because I climbed up there to see it. And I saw machine gun shell casings in the river where we used to go swimming.

Those images took me back to my first view of the aftermath of war. I know there are many people my age who have images like that sitting in a special filing drawer in their memory bank. The file name is "War" and I add to it films and pictures and stories of what I learn about what humans have done to each other over the centuries.

In the remembering, I became a bit emotional because I wanted to write about the first anniversary of the war in Ukraine, and those television pictures of the rubble in the streets and those huge apartment buildings scarred and blasted. Those little villages bombed to smithereens, with the elderly stumbling around with their worldly possessions in plastic bags, are more than disturbing.

And so here is what I thought I was going to say about this dastardly event. I wanted to know more about this chunk of the world. Some of it I knew, but doing the research and comparisons became even more shocking and riveting.

Ukraine is slightly smaller than Saskatchewan in area and 11 times larger than Nova Scotia. It is the second-largest country in Europe, after Russia. There were 46-million people there before the killing and exodus started last year.

The land mass of Ukraine has "belonged" to many over the centuries. It was one of the republics in the USSR not too long ago. The Tatars had a go at that piece of land, as did the Mongols. And then there was the Ottoman Empire. The Greeks held part of it 'way back then, too. It's a dizzying history. Someone always seemed to be claiming it or marching through it to get to somewhere else.

I had known about the huge emigration of Ukrainians in the 1930s—especially to Canada—when there was a famine caused by Stalin, some say to eliminate a Ukrainian independence movement.

Canada has the world's third-largest Ukrainian population, behind Ukraine itself and Russia. And Federal statistics show 167,585 Ukrainians have arrived in Canada by air or land since January 1, 2022.

As I was reading all these facts about this country which has been fortunate to have a charismatic, savvy and brave leader, I wish there was a way to stop the carnage and the ravaging of its countryside. Giving up does not seem to be an option for this country. To the question of figuring out what will stop the Russian leader without throwing all of Europe into another terrible full-scale war, I have no answer.

But we fly their flag here in support and hope the world can figure something out—soonest.

Immediacy

June 29. 2023

I may have mentioned that I'm a news junkie—not always a flattering term, but I watch a lot of news on television, and I read a lot of news online.

Last Saturday was unbelievable. I was glued to the news channels watching the events in Russia, as the mercenary Wagner Group seemed on the verge of toppling the government headed by Vladimir Putin[44]. Aside from the actual events, I was amazed at the speed we got what was

---

44 aljazeera.com/news/2023/6/24/timeline-how-wagner-groups-revolt-against-russia-unfolded

going on almost as it was happening. I'll leave all the machinations and the implications of what happened to the experts. I do have a couple of opinions, but I'll leave punditry to others.

We also watched and listened in horror to the news of that dreadful shipwreck in the Mediterranean Sea[45]. Those poor people who were trying to go somewhere else so they could have a life and being robbed to pay for an unbelievably awful escape route.

And then there was the submersible *Titan*, which imploded on its way to visit the wreck of the *Titanic*, with five rich folks on board[46]. There will be fallout from that episode, too.

And while all the above stories were certainly newsworthy, I was mostly struck by seeing and hearing about them almost immediately. The pictures and the reporters were on that screen with Breaking News right now.

I was thinking about the Reuters news article that appeared in *The Royal Gazette and Colonist* of Hamilton, Bermuda on Monday, February 12, 1945, telling the world that my Dad,

> wounded by flak after a strafing mission of Germany, thrown out of his cockpit and baling out into the slipstream, managed to drift back into the Allied lines and land on the doorstep of his favourite "pub" (tavern).

The event happened on January 16, 1945, so it took almost a month for the report to make it into the newspaper

I also thought about the time when I was watching TV in Chambly, Quebec, with my eldest daughter in her crib in the living room because she had a terrible case of chicken pox, I watched Walter Cronkite deliver the terrible news about President Kennedy having been assassinated in Texas. Then I saw the accused shooter, Lee Harvey, Oswald being shot live on TV[47].

I was glued to the TV for the next three days, watching the news almost as it happened.

All the television coverage of the Vietnam War showed people back in the United States what war was really like almost as it happened, fuelling the anti-war movement that made that war end. I do realize that it wasn't

---

45 wikipedia.org/wiki/2023_Messenia_migrant_boat_disaster
46 en.wikipedia.org/wiki/Titan_submersible_implosion
47 rarehistoricalphotos.com/jack-ruby-shot-oswald-1963/

quite as simple as that, but seeing those pictures every night on the tele-vision set certainly brought home how brutal war is.

I have over-simplified some of the above, but what we see nowadays is much more realistic and immediate than the reporting in the early part of the last century. But just because we can see and hear news sooner, doesn't make it any less horrific.

Climate Change

My husband is a science guy. He has been concerned about the changing climate and the damage we do to Gaia (the ancestral mother—sometimes parthenogenic—of all life).

Over the years we have tried to do the best we could with recycling, returning bottles for recycling, composting, all the responsible stuff. We were fortunate to be able to purchase an electric vehicle, which felt like the culmination of our bit to help reduce greenhouse gases. We still do all the other things as a matter of course.

Anne Crossman's

Electric vehicles

November 25, 2021

Sometimes we human beings need a real shock to our sensibilities to realize that "something" needs to be done. The weather nightmares that have hit British Columbia over this past year, with the dreadful heat, the subsequent fires and now the flooding of valleys, have focused the mind on the climate crisis.

What with all the discussions and not very satisfactory words coming out of that COP26 climate conference in Glasgow, Scotland in the past weeks, we decided to do our part and look at buying an EV—electric vehicle.

The discussion in our household probably is much the same in other homes around. It usually starts off with, "How much will it cost?"

And the, "Which manufacturer has the best reviews?"

This means a trip to the drug store to get a copy of *Consumer Reports*. After poring over the magazine for a week or so—not me, mind you—we discussed a couple of likely vehicles.

Then there's the vehicle we have now—a pretty good one which hasn't given us much grief over the seven years we've had it. It has 4-wheel drive, which we need in the winter to get up the driveway. The questions are:

> "Should we trade it in?"
> "Should we sell it privately?"
> "What will we get for it?"
> "Should we get an SUV or a hatchback?"

This discussion goes on for quite a few weeks before either of us actually talk to a dealership. The call is made. And we then hear from the dealership person every day for a week.

We ask questions:

Do you have a charging station?
Well, no, not yet...but soon.
Do you have a mechanic who knows how to fix an EV (we're learning the lingo)?
Well, no, not yet...but soon.

And then the final time we take a deep breath and actually drive into a dealership and ask the big question:

Do you have any EVs we can look at?
No, they won't be here for at least two years, and we don't have a charging station and we don't have an EV mechanic.

Now, I'm not griping about all this. And I'm certainly not whining about the dealerships. I'm quite sure that if we went further afield, we could find an EV and we could get the federal and provincial rebates which the car companies will have taken into account when they quote you the price. Which you will have to do some haggling over. Which is the way one buys vehicles.

It's all very well to have the EVs for sale in the urban centres with the charging stations and the qualified mechanics available, but think of all those commuters driving into those urban centres after hopefully charging their vehicles overnight out in the rural areas. Seems to me like we have that backwards.

Speaking of charging stations, an outfit called Electrify America has now "reached a milestone of 200 ultra-fast EV charging stations and over 830 individual charging stations" in California. Fourteen of the ultra-fast chargers are solar-powered.

We don't haggle well, we have learned—much to our chagrin—over the years. I have said in the past that if we ever have to buy a big item again, we need to take one particular friend and/or my sister-in-law with us. Boy, they sure know how to get a good deal.

Oh, yes, there is always looking at the hybrids, which have at least been around a bit longer and have a track record. Which means that we have to go back to that magazine.

Although it's terrific that we do the blue-bag recyclable thing, it's just not enough to change things in a way that will avert the climate crisis. Changing the way we live is going to be hard, and we all need to pick something concrete that we can afford to do. For each of us as individuals, and for our communities and country, it has to start somewhere.

Rise of sea level

September 8, 2022

Some information came out in the last while about "zombie ice". That sounded quite intriguing, to say the least. A glaciologist at the Geological Survey of Denmark and Greenland says this kind of ice is "dead" and will not grow because the parent glacier is not receiving enough snow.

It turns out that Greenland's ice sheet is melting at a rather quick rate. By the end of this century, this ice melt could raise the ocean level by 10.6 inches, or 26.9 cm. Although the oceans apparently don't all rise to the same level, that's quite a lot of extra water to be sloshing around. As the scientist adds, the above measurement doesn't take into account extra high tides or storm surges that come with hurricanes.

One report says that if that amount of water was concentrated over the United States, it would be 37 feet deep. Of course, it won't happen that way, but it does make one think.

And so, if we think of all the great cities on the edges of the continents and if we consider all the great deltas where farming takes place, it paints a grim picture.

I live on a rise above the Annapolis River. My altimeter says I am 75 feet above sea level. Given that the river is tidal up this far, I think the highway might be swamped.

While the Greenland ice is melting at a fast clip at the "top" of the planet, there is word that Thwaites Glacier attached to the South Pole ice is melting from the bottom up. That means that it will detach from the sea bottom and start moving away into warmer waters. Known as the "Doomsday Glacier" because of the ramifications of its loss, Thwaites is the widest in the world. It's 80 miles wide, and equal to about the size of Florida, It could raise sea levels by 10 feet all by itself, scientists say.

I note that the Town of Annapolis Royal has hired Atlantic Infrastructure Management Network to do a study on protecting its historic district. Much work has been done on gathering information; what is needed now is the solution. The town is to be commended for looking forward. I wish them well.

Being able to see what damage a warmer climate will have on one's home and one's province should be enough to remind us that every little bit helps in an effort to slow down climate warming.

Use less power. Try not to consume constantly. Don't buy things you don't need. See if you can afford to get an electric vehicle. Get off that oil furnace if you can. Grow your own veggies and fruit if you have the room on your property. Buy local food. It doesn't have to be trucked in from Quebec or California.

It will be a constant balance between what you want and what you need. I find myself asking if I really need to buy something and am telling myself that I can get another year out of whatever new piece of clothing that has caught my eye.

And don't think that 2050 is away in the future. It will be here before you know it.

Going electric for an important cause

December 1, 2022

It was time to get a new vehicle. We got the best out of our all-wheel-drive one over the past eight years. It was, of course, a gas vehicle.

It turns out that the man we have bought our two previous vehicles from has moved to Digby. On a trip to renew a driver's license there, a spur-of-the-moment run into one of the car dealerships found him again. What a surprise!

We sat in the showroom, talking shop. The salesman went out to bring a couple of vehicles to the front and I sat in one of them, looked the other one over. We went back into the office, and I said, "Get out your credit card for the deposit!"

We are now the proud owners of a 2023 Chevy Bolt EUV in Radiant Red Tintcoat, which is on its way from far away and could be here in a month or more. It will depend on the newly-throttled supply system, given the COVID restrictions and supply chain issues. I am hoping for a very red Christmas present.

We have wanted an electric vehicle for some time now. It seemed like a chance to put our money where our mouth was on the whole climate change discussion.

While I have not been as vocal as others, it seems to me that anything a person can do to help slow down carbon emissions, the better.

We are fortunate that we can afford to do this, I understand that. But it has to start somewhere, and every little bit helps

So my thinking goes like this: if you can afford it, take advantage of any or all of the government grants which are available to change the way you heat your home. Try to drive less by lumping all your driving to stores, appointments and so on into fewer trips.

Speaking of Christmas and presents, what a lovely time I had at the O'Dell House Museum in Annapolis Royal last week. I was asked to be a judge in the first Gingerbread House contest. I was amazed at the creativity, from the very young to the more mature folks. I do hope this is a tradition that will keep going through the years.

Last but not least, I have been watching the FIFA games. I must admit that I don't watch football (soccer) on a regular basis, but when it's a major tournament like the World Cup, that's another matter. The politics going on this year are interesting, but I really wanted to watch Canada.

And I did. The first Canadian FIFA goal ever—in the first two minutes—was amazing. The rest not so much. But it was fun to watch, and the team did well.

Fire and Brimstone

June 8, 2023

While this may be a bit of a stretch, the week just past made me think of fire and brimstone. Some might recall that phrase from the Bible. If not, here's what the Bible says:

> Then the Lord rained brimstone and fire on Sodom and Gomorrah, from the Lord out of the heavens.[48]

---

48   Genesis 19:24

I'm sure we remember hearing that Sodom and Gomorrah were very wicked places and I'll not go into all the sinning that went on there.

Somehow, humankind's sinning has been the use of Planet Earth. We have not been good stewards. While many of the inventive marvels have been useful over time, and especially in the past century, the cost to the earth has been horrendous.

Mouthing the words "climate change" and "climate crisis" doesn't really do very much, does it? While the preaching done by David Suzuki and Al Gore, to name a couple, has become shop-worn and repetitive, we should have paid more attention. Mostly, we should have actually done something.

Building more pipelines, churning up the oil sands, building refineries, fracking, pumping that so-called black gold needs to be shut down a lot sooner than is being done. Carbon capture is a false narrative. It implies that if we just pump that carbon back into the ground, we'll be fine. And then there's coal.

There are places where the Earth is being affected that we in Canada don't think of at all. The permafrost in that huge chunk of our country "up there" is melting. Two things come to mind: all those buildings built on pilings are starting to sink into the ground. And when that permafrost melts, all kinds of gases are being released—think methane gas. That is working its way into the atmosphere, adding to the carbon dioxide which is warming our planet at an alarming rate.

I am not a scientist. I don't have that kind of mind. So if I am actually paying attention to all this, my thinking says it must be pretty bad to have penetrated this non-scientific brain.

There is technology now that will help reduce carbon emissions. You know them—solar, wind, and tidal power. There are all kinds of subsidies being given to the oil and gas industry, it's been going on for years. If that money went into these new technologies, it would go a long way to getting us off the carbon-producing old technology.

I still have a hard time believing that coal is still being used to produce electricity. Surely the start of the so-called Industrial Age, and its choking, smog-ridden cities with people dying of lung diseases at an alarming rate and much younger than they ought to, should have taught us something.

Other familiar texts come to mind after this week of fire and brimstone but the one that sticks in my mind right now is "Ye reap what ye sow"[49].

PS - My thoughts go out to those in this province who have lost their homes to the immense fires. My admiration for the firefighters is unbounded.

PPS - I have actually done some paid work for the oil and gas industry in the past. I wanted to let you know that.

Those fires

August 24, 2023

I am the matriarch of a branch of our family that lives in Canada's North and British Columbia. I am so relieved to say that all are safe from the wildfires[50]. One branch of the branch lives in Yellowknife and, by happenstance, they were on vacation in BC with another branchlet. They had started their vacation before the evacuation order went out. Whew!

That BC branchlet is watching as smoke roils up behind the big hill just to the south of them. They all now have their bags packed and piled up next to the door.

I know the countryside around Yellowknife and have visited the country near Penticton, BC. I can see those billowing clouds of smoke in pictures as of right now and I know where they are.

While my mind is with all the people getting out of town already, or being ready to go at a moment's notice, I think of all those other people around the world who are leaving their homes because the droughts or the floods have become overwhelming.

And so we now have what someone called "climate refugees". Within Canada! Think about that! This is the country where refugees came seeking refuge, from all over the world. And now we have refugees in our own land.

---

49   Galatians 6:7
50   wikipedia.org/wiki/2023_Canadian_wildfires

I watched some golf last weekend, and it was being played just near Calgary. One of the announcers was going on about how much money this tournament had raised for charity. Millions, he said. And my first thought was, "Oil money." My second thought was wondering if that money was going to help the Northern refugees who might not have had to leave their homes if the oil industry had been throttled back years ago.

Last Sunday, Hurricane Hilary was downgraded to a tropical storm. That's not the big news. The big news is that this is an unheard-of storm hitting the west coast of North America. And in the middle of that, there was 5.1 magnitude earthquake in California.

The forest fires in Canada this year are breaking records. When your country has vast forests as we have, there are fires. They are caused mainly by lightning but are also caused, deliberately or not, by people.

Our household has started thinking about what we would take with us should we have to go somewhere in a hurry. We're whittling it down. It has given us a perspective on what is important and what we can do without.

And, yes, I am going on again about climate change, which in today's world has reached Climate Crisis status.

I do believe Gaia has just about had enough of us.

First Nations

Moving to the North of Canada was one of the best things I ever did. The vastness, the cold, the winters were there for sure. But I got to learn about Indigenous histories, their cultures and their attachment to their lands. I was able to carry that awareness with me through many places as I moved through the unceded territories to different parts of the country, including

- Prince Rupert, BC – Tsimshian
- Regina, SK – Cree
- La Ronge, SK – Cree
- Trenton and Ottawa, ON –Anishinaabeg Huron-Wendat, Algonquin
- Montreal, QC – The Kanien'kehá:ka (Mohawk) Nation
- Fredericton, NB – Wolastoqiyik, Mi'kmaq and Peskotomuhkati
- Nova Scotia – Mi'kmaq
- Newfoundland – Beothuk and Mi'kmaq
- Northwest Territories – Dene, Inuit, Inuvialuit and Métis
- Nunavut – Some of Nunavummiut land

Anne Crossman's

Residential Schools

June 10, 2021

There are many places to lay blame for this shameful piece of Canada's past, the oppression and mistreatment of the original peoples of our land. Residential schools are a big part of it. The deaths of their littles who were forced into those schools are shameful and horrendous.

It starts further back than these buildings in the smaller communities in our country. It starts with broken treaties, no rights, the punitive Indian Act, the politicians, the churches (there were more than one involved), the powerlessness of the First Nations for decades and decades, the immoral acts by people "in charge" and the "turning a blind eye" to the present situation on many of the reserves in some of the poorest real estate in our county.

We have a lot to answer for.

We have paid far more attention to what happened in the U.S. We were "educated" by those Saturday-afternoon movies about the poor people in the wagon trains getting attacked by "savages", and the belittling of First Nations people in those same films. You know the ones, I watched them, too, when I was a kid.

My learning about residential schools and the inter-generational damage they caused began many years ago when I lived in different Northern places in our country. I met the people whose families were trying to heal themselves after having their heritage taken from them. I met those people who battled on to retrieve the pride they had in living on the land and learning skills that kept them throughout tens of thousands of years in places we newcomers considered awful and backwoods and not-worth-living-in and too-hard-to-battle-the-elements. These places were "home" to the various communities of spirit.

During this Time of COVID, one of the pastimes that has consumed many is genealogy. People are looking for their ancestors, getting DNA tests to see where they came from, doing family trees, digging out old photographs and finding headstones in long-forgotten cemeteries all over the world.

Imagine looking for your ancestors when a whole generation was ripped out, leaving a blank section on your family tree. Imagine knowing a family member who can't speak about a whole section of his/her life because it is too painful.

I know where I came from, I have "met" many of my ancestors through birth and death certificates, passenger lists, newspaper articles, photographs, diaries, and headstones in graveyards.

Just imagine you are a mother and father living in Fort Good Hope on the Mackenzie River in the Northwest Territories and the RCMP come to the dock and try to tell you that they have to take your son and daughter away to go to school. You don't speak English or French. The RCMP do not speak Slavey. You get a piece of paper. The priest/minister tells you that this is the right thing to do.

You never see your children again—ever. You have no idea where they went. Your world consists of a huge piece of land where you hunt and fish and make a living. You don't know about big cities; you only know of "schooling" as a way to teach your children how to live on the land that their Creator gave them.

The unspeakable stories told to the Truth and Reconciliation Commission (TRC)[51] are not all that could be revealed. Some didn't want their stories made public.

The tears and anguish and methods of dealing with all that have echoed through a couple of generations now. I listened to what the Honourable Murray Sinclair, the chair of the TRC has said about the Commission's work and its findings. Please look for his words. They are vital. Please talk to your MP about "doing" something instead of sending out the usual platitudes.

We all need to try to help a group of our fellow citizens who absolutely need us to do so.

---

51 thecanadianencyclopedia.ca/en/article/truth-and-reconciliation-commission

Calls to action

July 1, 2021

Last week, the media broadcast news of the cemetery near a Saskatchewan residential school. It was followed by a couple of interviews with an old friend of mine from Northern days, Marie Wilson. Marie lives in Yellowknife. She was one of the three commissioners on the Truth and Reconciliation Commission (TRC).

Their final report came out in December of 2015[52]. She was angry and sad during those interviews. She read from Volume 4 of that final report, demonstrating that the information about the deaths of these children at the residential schools was there for all to see.

I will add that the people in charge of the schools knew about these tragic, and probably lonely, deaths all those years ago. The families of these children may not have known. Those families were left with imagining the worst. The parents may not have been informed why their children never came home.

Moving back to present day, or at least 2015, why were we not outraged when the TRC brought out its report? Are we so inured to tragedy that Volume 4 just slid by without a mention? Why did it take the shocking numbers of 215 unmarked graves, and then 751, to take hold and grip the media and now the world?

Worth reading is a report by Dr. Scott Hamilton, a professor in the Department of Anthropology at Lakehead University in Thunder Bay, who worked from 2013-15 identifying Residential-School-related gravesites across Canada. His full report, *Where are the Children buried?* was made public only following Chief Casimir's (the Chief of the Kamloops Indian Band) announcement on May 27, 2021. Hamilton said in an interview with *The B.C. Catholic* that he believes his study "provides important de-

---

52   rcaanc-cirnac.gc.ca/eng/1450124405592/1529106060525. The National Centre for Truth and Reconciliation has continued the Commission's work, and has issued many more reports, which are available at nctr.ca

tail and context for a public grappling with the implications of the Kamloops news."

The irony about the above quote, dated June 3, 2021, is that it is from *The B.C. Catholic:* "a weekly publication serving the needs of the Catholic community in British Columbia. It is the official newspaper of the Archdiocese of Vancouver."

I recommend reading this report if you are not prepared to read the five volumes of the TRC report[53]. Dr. Hamilton's work, along with the work of many others, contributed to the TRC.

As time goes on this year, we will, no doubt, hear of more of these terrible legacies of a racist and colonialist past in our country. These little graves remind us of what was here in Canada. Let them also be a lesson in what the term "systemic racism" means. Let us remind ourselves that this history is what brought us to today and I hope makes us understand our fellow human beings better.

This Canada Day will not be like others we have had over the years. The pandemic has cast a pall over things again this year and these terrible revelations make things even worse. Let us try to do better.

And to my friend Marie: continue to be strong and advocate on behalf of all those little ones and their families.

Truth and Reconciliation Commission
some of the Calls to Action

Missing Children and Burial Information

71. We call upon all chief coroners and provincial vital statistics agencies that have not provided to the Truth and Reconciliation Commission of Canada their records on the deaths of Aboriginal children in the care of residential school authorities to make these documents available to the National Centre for Truth and Reconciliation.

72. We call upon the federal government to allocate sufficient resources to the National Centre for Truth and Reconciliation to allow it to develop and maintain the National Residential School Student Death Register established by the Truth and Reconciliation Commission of Canada.

---

53 ehprnh2mwo3.exactdn.com/wp-content/uploads/2021/05/AAA-Hamilton-cemetery-FInal.pdf

73. We call upon the federal government to work with churches, Aboriginal communities, and former residential school students to establish and maintain an online registry of residential school cemeteries, including, where possible, plot maps showing the location of deceased residential school children.

74. We call upon the federal government to work with the churches and Aboriginal community leaders to inform the families of children who died at residential schools of the child's burial location, and to respond to families' wishes for appropriate commemoration ceremonies and markers, and reburial in home communities where requested.

75. We call upon the federal government to work with provincial, territorial, and municipal governments, churches, Aboriginal communities, former residential school students, and current landowners to develop and implement strategies and procedures for the ongoing identification, documentation, maintenance, commemoration, and protection of residential school cemeteries or other sites at which residential school children were buried. This is to include the provision of appropriate memorial ceremonies and commemorative markers to honour the deceased children.

76. We call upon the parties engaged in the work of documenting, maintaining, commemorating, and protecting residential school cemeteries to adopt strategies in accordance with the following principles:

> i. The Aboriginal community most affected shall lead the development of such strategies.

> ii. Information shall be sought from residential school Survivors and other Knowledge Keepers in the development of such strategies.

> iii. Aboriginal protocols shall be respected before any potentially invasive technical inspection and investigation of a cemetery site.

Mary May Simon

July 15, 2021

I would like to express my sincere appreciation and thank everyone for all your well wishes and kind words and support for my appointment as the new Governor General for Canada.

Nakurmiimarialuk ilunnasie allaqatatusie uvanut tillijauniri-lauqtara pitjutrilugu Prime Minister Trudeau-mut.

– Mary Simon, July 8, 2021

The news about the impending investiture of the 30th Governor General of Canada was astounding for me, as it was for many others, I am sure. I distinctly remember saying—out loud—when the previous GG blotted her copybook and bowed out, that "they" should pick Mary Simon.

Like many are saying these days, I met Mary long ago. She was in Inuvik for the Inuit Circumpolar Conference. Her husband, Whit Fraser, our longtime family friend, was with her. I have read about Mary's quiet feats of negotiation and diplomacy for years. Anyone who has spent time in Northern Canada knows of her career. And they know her husband's CBC career. They are what would be called today a "power couple".

They are, however, an unassuming couple you would love to invite to your party. (This is my gauge of people: if I would like them in my home or in the backyard for a party, then they must be all right.)

Actually, Whit has been in our backyard, and he has slept in our guest room. He was here in June, 2019 as a speaker at our Ernest Buckler Literary Event Society *Reading Where We Live* event. He was a big hit. He told stories about the North and quoted from his book *True North Rising.* The audience was enthralled, and I don't use that word lightly.

So here we are in 2021 and we are going to have an Inuk lady as our Governor General. There are some who say we should be doing away with this office and cutting our ties with the British monarchy. If that happens, let it not be before Mary May Simon has put in her five years

and helped with the reconciliation process that absolutely needs to happen in our country. She will be a gracious, firm and kind leader who will
help us through the next rocky times.

In this Time of COVID, this announcement was a ray of hope. I have
heard others say the same thing. I cannot think of a better person for this
job. And with Whit living in Rideau Hall, there will be laughter and
twinkling eyes. What a combo!

Governor General Mary Simon. Photo: Sgt
Johanie Maheu, Rideau Hall

PS—People in Annapolis Royal may now have an idea of what it's been
like for all those Indigenous communities in Canada who have either had
no water or have had to boil their water for years and years.

Anne Crossman's

Thundermakers!

July 7, 2022

There is something about the drum. For me, it gets into my very bones. And it reminds me of so many places and people I have met and known in our country.

I have been thrilled by Inuit drum dancers in Rankin Inlet in Nunavut, Inuvialuit drum dancers in Inuvik, Tsimshian drummers and dancers in Prince Rupert, the Dene drummers in Yellowknife and now the Mi'kmaq Thundermakers here in Annapolis Royal.

I went to see Alan Syliboy and the Thundermakers at King's Theatre last weekend. The music was a wonderful harmony of voices, instruments, and the drums. The visuals were very moving and matched the songs—a blending of Alan Syliboy's art and the petroglyphs of Kejimkujik.

And all the while that big drum was throbbing.

And, to add to the drama of the evening, they performed in Annapolis Royal, where the first Mi'kmaq Peace and Friendship Treaty was signed in 1726. Seventy-seven Indigenous male delegates signed the first part of the treaty, and the second part was signed by the colony's principal military leaders, Lawrence Armstrong and John Doucett. Armstrong was the Lieutenant-Governor of Nova Scotia while Doucett was the Lieutenant-Governor of the British garrison at Annapolis Royal.

The spoken word pieces by Syliboy were warm and observant of our planet but warning that we need to treat our planet better, and with care.

Hubert Francis played guitar and sang a couple of his songs about his life journey. Syliboy's son Evan played an amazing guitar; Matt Gallant on drums was terrific; and Joanne Hadfield's vocals, along with guitar, flute, piano and percussion, were spellbinding. Lukas Pearce put together the images that flickered behind the performers.

I know, I used a lot of over-worked adjectives above, but I'll bet you dollars to donuts that the people in the audience would agree with every one. The theatre boomed with applause and then rhythmic clapping to bring the group back on stage for an encore.

To get a taste of what this remarkable ensemble is about, here is a link to a video that was done with Symphony Nova Scotia: www.youtube.-

com/watch?v=WsJsHq62Tck.

Syliboy said of this performance that he was delighted with the chance to play with the orchestra.

If you ever get a chance to go to a concert with these fine musicians, go.

Teaching and learning another culture

October 6, 2022

Watching the ceremonies around the country on Truth and Reconciliation Day last week reminded me of the Indigenous teachers I have known.

These teachers were not in any school I attended. They didn't live where I grew up. I learned from my colleagues and friends in my travels around Canada during my time with CBC.

One of the first teachers was in La Ronge in Northern Saskatchewan, Allan, a young man from Black Lake near Uranium City. He is Chipewyan. He speaks his language. I worked with him at CBC. He went on the CBC airwaves for four years there and then went on to CBC in Yellowknife. And then became a leader in various places back in his home province. He taught me resilience and pride in his culture.

And there was my Inuk mentor in Rankin Inlet, Jose Kusugak. When I landed there to do my job interview, I was met by a driver with a small pickup truck and taken to the local hotel. Good thing, I wore reasonable clothes, as I rode in the back of that truck.

While I don't always follow my own advice, I did tell myself that I should keep my eyes and ears open, and my mouth shut for at least six months so I could learn.

I made the cut and started work in a small building with five Inuit and one other Qablunaaq (white person). That building was one of the older ones in town. Every time the blizzard wind blew, the corner office in the back would lift up and sink down, like a ship in a storm.

My best memory from that job was being exasperated with some CBC bureaucratic rule being broken, and Jose would tell me to get a cup of coffee, come in to his office, and close the door. There, he would give me cross-cultural lesson number 342. By the time the coffee was gone, I was mesmerized, the exasperation had evaporated, and I was smiling when I opened the door. He was so generous and patient. I tried to be a sponge.

I learned from the Gwich'in staff who worked at the CBC Radio station in Inuvik. And I learned from the Inuvialuit staff at the same location.

I learned about their residential school stories—there was one of those schools in Inuvik. I heard the stories of the destruction of that generation's culture. I also learned about those elders who insisted that the culture not be lost. I heard the stories that were handed down from generation to generation. Those stories were sent out over the CBC airwaves, so we were a small part of helping those cultural memories survive.

There was a contingent of young CBC on-air people who came from the South to get experience, so they thought, so they could go down South and get into one of the big CBC stations. They did move on, but they learned and took more than broadcasting knowledge with them when they did eventually move on with their lives.

When I look back on my time in mid-North and Northern Canada, I am forever grateful to all those Indigenous people who gave their knowledge freely and helped me to understand what they were up against when the Europeans moved in.

I owe them a debt of gratitude I will never be able to repay.

My Favourites

I expect anyone who has done any writing has some favourite pieces. They are the ones that give the author both satisfaction and pleasure because "it" came out right and the people who read "it" got it right away and told the author.

This last section is for those. I knew what I wanted to say, did so and heard from readers that they agreed, had the same kind of experience, wished they had known, and told me so.

Anne Crossman's

Olympics: astounding

August 5, 2021

Here are some random thoughts on this year's Olympics, from an inveterate watcher. I watch them all, sometimes in the middle of the night and sometimes over lunch. I usually don't watch sporting events the rest of the time—well, maybe golf in the middle of winter so I can see green grass.

I am a sluggard when it comes to personal sports. I remember, rather vaguely, that I used run in school meets, play softball at lunch breaks in school and swim.

The Olympic events are special, though. The efforts that those people put in to be the best in their chosen event are astounding. The ages when they started training are amazing. The focus is stunning. I have none of these attributes, it is clear.

There have been a few blemishes on all this joy this year. The one that has really got to me is the costumes the women volleyball players wear. Why they wear those bikinis is a bit unclear at the moment. Some people want to have someone to blame. I find the whole thing distasteful and from the 1950s. Surely, we have moved on in 2021.

I have mixed feelings about the professional versus "true" amateur discussion. And I have mixed thoughts on Qatar recruiting its team entries from around Africa. I do remember the discussions that raged when the hockey teams were to be made up of NHL players. The whole question of money always makes things murkier.

The first modern Olympic games were held in 1896, and the first women entered in 1900. Wikipedia says, "22 women competed at the 1900 Games, 2.2% of all the competitors. Alongside sailing, golf and tennis, women also competed in croquet." I think croquet has dropped out of the picture.

Now back to this year's 2020 games, which are, of course, actually taking place in 2021. The history books will have fun explaining this one. The delight that shows on the athletes' faces when they do their best and actually win is heart-warming. The body shapes are kind of fascinating, too. These long, lean, inverted triangular shapes of swimmers are certainly cut out to do the sport they have chosen.

Since all women under the age of 21 have never cut their hair (think Rapunzel), there have been some wild-looking hairdos, especially under the bathing caps. The dye jobs on some of the athletes' hair is pretty spectacular, too.

The ego and self-awareness that must be required to do these feats are ginormous. There were all kinds of demonstrations of that characteristic. I feel for the women in gymnastics who were injured, either physically or mentally. I just can't imagine what it must feel like to be in the middle of the air and not know where you are or what you are supposed to do next. Simone Biles describing the feeling as "the twisties" is pretty horrifying. I'm glad she withdrew. That alone takes guts beyond something I can visualize.

Watching Andre de Grasse on Sunday running his personal best at 9.89 seconds in the 100-metre dash was just great. I could hear the cheers from across the country.

As we watch the closing ceremony of this year's Summer Olympics on Saturday, I want to remember the effort these events took, and my admiration goes out to all.

Celebrating Ernest Buckler

July 20. 2023

I wonder what Ernest Buckler would have thought about the event that took place at the West Dalhousie Community Hall last Saturday? One thing I'm pretty sure about—he would not have been there. He might have been sitting out in his car, though, wondering what we were saying about him.

The Ernest Buckler Literary Event Society held its fifth gathering to celebrate an author who was born in West Dalhousie. In 1954 he broke the mould of Canadian authors who wrote about city life.

The Mountain and the Valley has been read by millions over the years.

It is studied in universities. There is a half-hour docudrama based on the book, produced over ten years ago. Margaret Atwood met him when she was young.

I won't go on and on here, but know that this guy, who was born in West Dalhousie, wrote much of his work in a back room of a house in Centrelea.

When the various societies over the years felt they should "do one more event", COVID-19 came along. So our bi-annual (every two years) plan went down the drain.

The theme of our events was *Reading Where We Live*. We wanted to celebrate authors who wrote about the places they know and the people who lived there. And so this year we had some of the best of Canadian authors, a local singer-songwriter and a local raconteur.

These people took us to rural Ontario in sugarbush country, and they took us to the high Canadian Arctic and to the Nova Scotia countryside. We also heard a wistful story with a few tears woven in, written by Ern.

My job was to introduce two of our guests and to close out the program. I have learned much about this shy man since I started working on the first event in 2008. Ern's first cousin once removed said he was "extremely smart" and therefore considered "a bit odd" by the other kids. He went to Bridgetown High School and wrote his provincial exams. He was 12. One winter, the teacher in Dalhousie became ill and Ern took over and taught the school for the rest of that year. He was 13.

Our two out-of-town writers were Elizabeth Hay and Whit Fraser. Liz is a Giller prize winner (*Late Nights on Air*) with a number of books under her belt. Whit was here four years ago and talked about his life in the Northwest Territories, and this time he talked about his new novel set in the years after World War I and when the RCMP were sent North to keep our sovereignty alive.

These two people worked in Yellowknife when my husband worked at CBC Northern Service and I worked at the local weekly newspaper, *News of the North*. It was like old home week.

Kim Doolittle sang some of her great songs that evoked our place, and Ken Maher read one of Ern's short stories.

Here is the best description I know about Ernest Buckler. It's a quote from another Nova Scotia author, Harry Bruce, in a review Harry did of Claude Bissell's book *Ernest Buckler Remembered*.

> In a scholarly but affectionate tribute to his remarkable friend, Claude Bissell not only shows us why Ernest Buckler was a great

writer, but also reveals him as tough and thin-skinned, cranky and warm, funny and miserable, and all in all, as tortured and lovable a genius as Canadian literature has ever produced.

As we sat comfortably in the hall, listening to all these fascinating people, it occurred to me that the building was once a school which had been moved to the present site and had a couple of pieces built onto it. Buildings burn down, too, so I'm not sure about this, but I really want to believe that this hall that housed our event was the school that Ern attended and then taught in when he was just 13.

Before he became so famous in Canadian literary circles.

No book is a waste of its writer's time

August 31, 2023

A small group of folks were at a gathering recently. We were there to talk and listen about writing. I was struck by a question one person asked all of us: "Is the world really ready for a book about my memoirs?"

I think we were a bit taken aback; I know I was.

Writing is a kind of mysterious process. It's hard to describe. People who write poetry or novels or histories or stories about family history or children's stories or long letters home or long love letters or radio scripts or film scripts or stage plays will tell you they really don't quite know how it happens. What they *can* tell you is that the piece of writing has been churning around in their mind for some time. They'll tell you that a subject or random thought or a few key words in a conversation that stick in that filing cabinet in our heads and pop out just when you sit down to the keyboard (that's me).

I come from a long line of letter writers. I am fortunate to have letters written to me from my great aunt and my grandmother when I was very little. My mother wrote letters every day to friends and relatives. I have some of them. I moved out when I was 19 and my family always lived somewhere else for the rest of my life, so we kept in touch by letter.

My mother was a reader. I got books for Christmas and birthdays. Books were places to go to share an adventure or make a new friend.

Those who read this column know how delighted I was to have a book printed for my family about my father's and mother's time in England during the World War II[54]. I had enough copies made for family and the occasional friend. I still look at that book with my name on the spine with great delight.

I am really envious of those people who have the discipline and foresight to keep a diary—every day. Even if it was an ordinary day with nothing more exciting to write about than brushing your teeth, you will

---

54　See page 36.

be delighted when you go back and read the entries. I wish I had done more. My memories are a tad sketchy now and I probably have lost some good stories.

Just think what fun the grandkids will have when they read about how you got your first computer and had to exchange the floppy disks for practically everything. And remember DOS? See, that's what happens when you start remembering things.

So when the person asked if the world needed a book about his memoirs, I answered with a resounding Yes. No book is a waste of its author's time. It may not be a best-seller. It may not make oodles of moolah. But someone in the future might pick that book up and get a cup of tea or even something stronger, sit by a fire and open that book and settle in to share the life of someone they don't know but who thought it was a good idea to record the interesting things that happened in their life.

And late in the night, that reader will finish the last page, put the empty cup down, scratch their head and say, "What an interesting life this guy led! What interesting places he went to and people he met."

And that alone is worth the effort.

The torment of grant writing

September 7, 2023

I have given myself a stern lecture to never write another grant proposal again in whatever is left of my life.

It is possibly the most frustrating, soul-destroying, gnashing-of-teeth process sent to volunteer and not-for-profit organizations that I can imagine.

I have heard others—reasonable, smart people—say the same thing and even worse.

Here are the most egregious sins committed against us folks pounding away at their keyboard answering the same question put in 15 different ways—one suspects it is made to bulk up the form and make it look more important.

First, one fills in the name, address, phone number, and email addresses of at least three people in the organization, etc. By the way, this item is in there because most volunteer groups are run by old people so "they" want to get in touch (eventually) with someone still amongst us.

Then "they" want all kinds of information on your reason for being. And then the budget, which is sometimes right up there with dancing on the head of a pin.

There's a lot more stuff required as well. And then the PDF (which format, by the way, is a wretched invention by someone who thinks it prevents a documents from being modified after the creator has written it, or they just learned how to do it and figure everyone should learn how to do it, too) is sent off to who knows whom or where.

One could have run three marathons, climbed Mount Everest, had another grandchild, got divorced and remarried before one gets any inkling that "they" got your response to their pathetic excuse for a handout. Sometimes "they" ask a few more "clarifying" questions about the finished product or that wretched budget.

Oh yes, there's the timing. One has to wait patiently until "they" decide when one can submit said proposal. Then one has to figure out how long it's going to take to get the work done or whatever. And, don't forget, it all has to be completed by that March 31 doomsday date.

So I thought I might put together a short, easily-followed list for the "they" who might have some moolah to dole out.

1. Make the date to submit a proposal a reasonable amount of time ahead of the decision date.
2. When "they" receive a request, send a short note saying it was received and will be read. If there are questions, ask them promptly.
3. Tell the requester when they can expect an answer Yes or No, and state a reasonable amount of time—two months would be good.
4. Be very clear what projects are eligible for this grant.
5. Make the final report from the group the kind of report that makes them proud to have accomplished the project with the help given by your organization.

As an aside, the organizations "they" are dealing with drive the economy in small communities in ways that can't be measured the way you measure sales and revenues at the liquor commission. A nice certificate for volunteers, which is given to old folks across the country, is one thing, but dealing with those who extend themselves to help make their com-

Anne Crossman's

munity a nice place and a friendly place and an interesting place is worth a lot more.

Anne Crossman's

About the author

Anne M. (Tripe) Crossman has worked for newspapers and radio over the years—newspapers in Halifax, Bridgewater, Yellowknife and now the Annapolis Valley. She has worked for CBC Radio across the country—Newfoundland, Nova Scotia, New Brunswick, Saskatchewan, and the Northwest Territories.

While she has worked in other areas like economic development, writing has always been in the background—writing letters, journals, intermittent diaries and columns every week for the past three and a half years. This has been a great delight. Volunteering in her communities has kept her mind busy as well.

She now lives with her husband, Bill, in Annapolis Royal, Nova Scotia which is fitting, given her name.